dash

inspired kosher recipes for the seasoned palate

created by
Rebecca Naumberg and Sori Klein

a publication by torah academy for girls, far rockaway, new york

For additional copies or further information please call Torah Academy for Girls (718) 471-8444.

ISBN# 9780981519821
Library of Congress Control Number: 2011938204

Distributed by:
The Judaica Press, Inc.
123 Ditmas Avenue
Brooklyn, NY 11218

Ph: 800-972-6201 | 718-972-6200

info@judaicapress.com
www.judaicapress.com

Photographed & Printed by Albert Hakim, Laserwave Graphics • 732.745.7764 • www.laserwave.com

table of contents

appetizers

soups

salads

fish

poultry

meat

sides

bread & dairy

desserts

בס"ד

TORAH ACADEMY FOR GIRLS

בית יעקב ד' לאנג איילנד - *The Bais Yaakov of Long Island*

Dear Friends:

It is with a true sense of pride that we introduce the new TAG cookbook to you. No doubt, many of you who have enjoyed our previous cookbook, *Sharing Our Best*, are eager to add these tasteful recipes to your menus.

This beautiful cookbook is a testimony to two individuals who graciously "shared their best," who used their determination and talents to produce a cookbook which will help women prepare gourmet meals in an easy and efficient manner. I am hard pressed to find the right words to convey my appreciation to **Mrs. Rebecca Naumberg & Mrs. Sori Klein**, who so capably spearheaded this major undertaking. Much *hakaras hatov* is also due to all the women who gave of their time, talents and resources to make the dream of an updated cookbook a reality.

The art of cooking and preparing healthy and tasty dishes is a valuable asset in a woman's role as a nurturer. Many a mother and daughter have forged a solid bond by working together in the kitchen and preparing special foods for the Shabbos and Yom Tov table. Food plays a pivotal role in our lifestyle as Yidden. From the first *brachah* that we make before taking a bite until our Birkas Hamazon, we are always aware of the pivotal role Hashem plays in providing sustenance for us.

We at TAG have, *baruch Hashem*, also been fortunate to find a successful recipe to help produce a quality Bas Yisroel, who in turn will transmit all she has acquired to the next generation. As we build upon our past successes and look forward to educating thousands of young ladies, we are aware of the major ingredients that go into our finished products. We are truly grateful to our parent body for entrusting us with their most precious possessions, to our devoted staff of Principals and teachers who add just the right amount of knowledge, *hashkafah* and inspiration, and of course, to the Ribono Shel Olam, the true Creator of us all.

We are confident you will all enjoy this cookbook and that it will become a valuable addition to your culinary library.

Enjoy!

Rabbi Meyer Weitman
Dean

foreword

With tremendous appreciation for all the סיעתא דשמיא we have experienced, we are honored to present DASH to you. We believe that the recipes included in this cookbook will enhance your Shabbos and Yom Tov tables and be enjoyed for many years to come.

We would like to express our deep gratitude to our school, Torah Academy for Girls (TAG). The talent and care that the administration and teachers put into each and every student is extraordinary. We are truly fortunate to have such a remarkable staff that puts its collective hearts and souls into our girls. This cookbook is our way of giving back.

The origins and initiative for this cookbook started several years ago while we served as presidents of the Women's League. We were looking for ways to raise money for our school. Ideas slowly began to take shape, which segued into the project of producing a sequel cookbook to the wonderful, original TAG cookbook, Sharing Our Best. Whereas Sharing Our Best featured a selection of recipes contributed totally by our parent body, DASH presents gourmet and exotic recipes from our private collection, which were developed and perfected over the years, as well as delicious and unique recipes from other women. All recipes in DASH were tried and tested by volunteer cooks, and all photographs accurately depict each dish.

The title of our cookbook, DASH, feels appropriate in a number of ways. It brings to mind the "mad DASH through life" that we all seem to be speeding through. We sometimes have to slow ourselves down and appreciate the good that we, *baruch Hashem*, do have. We have included many quick and easy recipes, and tips for busy mothers, yielding elegant results that may appear to be time consuming but are really ready in a flash — or a DASH. We have incorporated a DASH of spice in our mouth-watering recipes to make them tasty and delectable.

As you read through the recipes, you will notice that many of them feature a "Simplify" feature. This is for when you just don't have the time necessary to devote to the full recipe and would love a tried and true shortcut. We have also offered plating tips and serving suggestions to help you plan your menus and decorate your tables.

Countless hours were spent planning the recipes, layout, visual details and format for this project and we are extremely pleased by the end result. Each recipe was professionally photographed, and the final product is far better than even we could have imagined.

This project was a daunting undertaking, which required a tremendous amount of research and effort. We have numerous people to thank as we could not have accomplished our goals without their help. Thank you to everyone who contributed their time, effort, recipes and ideas to make this cookbook as beautiful as it is.

 TAG is currently in the process of a major building project, and we hope that the proceeds from the sale of this cookbook will assist them in their endeavor. Please enjoy the delicious and beautiful recipes in our new TAG cookbook, DASH — and please help spread the word!

Rebecca Naumberg and Sori Klein

We gratefully acknowledge the wonderful women who contributed their time and energy to make this cookbook a reality. Our appreciation goes to those who generously submitted their treasured recipes, tested and perfected the dishes, and graciously provided their homes for photo shoots. We regret that only some of the recipes could be included in the cookbook, and hope that no volunteers have been inadvertently omitted from this list.

Special thanks to the following women who have devoted their time and knowledge selflessly and have really made this cookbook happen.

Naomi Ross, *recipe writing and editing*
Batsheva Golding, *layout and design*
Kiki Haas, *assisted in recipe creation, testing and plating*

Soshie Hirth, *TAG Women's League*
Mrs. Tzivia Schwartz, *photographer and use of her home*
Gitty Spilzinger, *assisted in recipe creation, testing and plating*

The TAG Cookbook would like to thank the dedicated staff of Gourmet Glatt Emporium for their generosity, helpfulness, and courteous service while we shopped and cooked for our photo shoots.

Mendy Herz
Howie Klagsbrun
Berel Wolowik, *meat dept. manager and his entire staff*
Ziggy Kohn, *produce manager and his entire staff*
Miriam Davila, *head cashier, cashiers and baggers*

Shloy Rubenstein
Yaakov Hagler
Chap a Nosh, *for their generous donation of food*
Schwartz's Appetizing, *for their generous donation of food*

Recipe Typing
Esther Friedman
Rivky Plaut

Editing
Chief Editor, Naomi Ross
Shani Belsky
Layella Bobker
Hadassah Goldsmith
Michelle Justic
Miriam Lichtman
Devora Lowy

Food Gemach
Aliza Gold

Layout and Design
Batsheva Golding

Cookbook Flyer
Dassy Weiss

Photoshoot Home
Evy & Zevi Guttman

Recipes
Rivky Bajnon
Alisa Berger
Hadassa Bobker
Leah Brecher
Devora Cywiack
Aliza Katz
Mindy Glaser
Tamar Gluck
Eileen Gross
Kiki Haas
Esther Hamada
Aviva Rosen
Aliza Katz
Rivky Keilson
Ruthy Klagsburn
Surie Klein
Mom's Pastries
Devora Monczyk
Mimi Nelkenbaum
Yona Oppenden
Mimi Oratz
Atara Perl
Avi Pifko
Tzippy Puterbeutel
The Prime Grill
Aviva Rosen
Ronit Schwartz

Shonie Schwartz
Goldie Sebrow
Blimi Weiss
Lauren Zuckerman

Platers
Carole Braunstein
Bukie Cohen
Goldy Fein
Suri Greenwald
Evy Guttman
Kiki Haas
Aviva Rosen
Chani Jacobowitz
Danielle Jacobs
Breindy Jacobson
Hindy Klaus
Miriam Lichtman
Rifka Mandel
Nina Meyer
Aviva Pifko
Dena Rogoff
Aviva Rosen
Ronit Schwartz
Gitty Spilzinger
Aliza Spinner
Osna Wasser

Cooks
Rivky Bajnon
Shani Belsky
Chaya Bernstein
Gitty Bodner
Carole Braunstein
Tzippy Charlop
Devora Cywiack
Devoiry Davidson
Devora Dreifus
Goldy Fein
Tamar Gluck
Aliza Gold
Suri Greenwald
Kiki Haas
Racheli Hahn
Gila Henesh
Aviva Rosen
Rena Hershkowitz
Shani Hirsch
Esther Holzberg
Chani Jacobowitz
Breindy Jacobson
Sara Leya Katz
Rivky Keilson
Ruthy Klagsburn
Tami Landy
Aviva Mendlowitz
Nina Meyer
Devora Monczyk

Deena Muller
Naomi Newman
Bruchie Norensberg
Aviva Pifko
Tzippy Puderbeutel
Paghit Ralbag
Aviva Rosen
Aliza Rosenberg
Devora Rubin
Shonie Schwartz
Ronit Schwartz
Chaya Scott
Goldie Sebrow
Tova Singer
Gitty Schonkopf
Gitty Spilzinger
Aliza Spinner
Chaya Ungar
Osna Wasser
Suri Weinreb
Ilana Wolberg
Nechama Zand

Coordinating
Faigy Hertz
Rivky Plaut
Sharon Shtern

Marketing Consultant
Zipi Lisker

appetizers

black and white chilean sea bass balls with pink grapefruit salad

For a magnificent starter course, these elegant baked sea bass balls have a light, sweet flavor that is accented by the tangy, bright pink grapefruit salad.

prep time
15-20 minutes

cook time
20 minutes plus freezing and thawing time

serves
6-8

- 2 tablespoons canola oil
- 1 small onion (¼ cup), finely minced
- 4 tablespoons cornstarch, divided
- 1 cup unsweetened coconut milk
- 1 pound Chilean sea bass, skinned and cut into very small cubes

- 1 teaspoon salt
- 1 cup panko bread crumbs
- 3 tablespoons mixed white and black sesame seeds
- 4 large egg whites, lightly beaten
- Pink Grapefruit Salad (*recipe below*)

Form sea bass balls: Line a large rimmed baking sheet with parchment paper. In a medium saucepan, heat oil over low heat. Add onion and sauté until softened, about 6 minutes. In a small bowl, whisk 2 tablespoons cornstarch into coconut milk until smooth. Add to onion and cook over medium-high heat, whisking, until bubbling and thick, about 2 minutes. Remove from heat and let cool to room temperature. Stir in sea bass and salt. Roll rounded tablespoons of mixture into 20 small balls. Place balls on the baking sheet. Cover and freeze until firm, about 1 hour.

Coat: In a medium bowl, toss panko bread crumbs with sesame seeds. In another medium bowl, whisk egg whites with remaining cornstarch until smooth. Dip frozen fish balls into egg mixture, letting any excess drip off. Dredge balls in panko bread crumb mixture to coat thoroughly. Return balls to the baking sheet, about 2 inches apart, and let stand at room temperature until thawed but not too soft (about 10 minutes).

Bake: Preheat oven to 350°. Bake balls for about 20 minutes or until golden brown. If not serving immediately, store balls, tightly covered, in the refrigerator. Reheat gently, uncovered.

Assemble salad: Place endives in a salad bowl or divide onto individual plates. Mound grapefruit over endives and serve. Top with sea bass balls.

pink grapefruit salad

- ¾ cup sugar
- ¼ cup lemon juice
- ¼ cup fresh ginger, peeled and finely grated
- 4 pink grapefruits

- 1 green chile pepper, minced (for less heat, use ½ of the pepper)
- 2 tablespoons soy sauce
- 8 endives, finely chopped

Ginger syrup: In a small saucepan, combine sugar, lemon juice and ginger. Bring to a boil over medium-high heat, stirring until sugar dissolves. Strain into a small bowl. Mix in chile pepper and soy sauce.

Grapefruit: Peel grapefruits with a sharp knife, removing all bitter white pith. Cut between membranes to release grapefruit sections. Transfer sections to a fine strainer over a large bowl and let stand for 15 minutes to drain off as much juice as possible. Discard juice and transfer grapefruit sections to the bowl. Gently toss with 6 tablespoons ginger syrup and let stand for 5 minutes.

squared pizzetta with capers

prep time
15 minutes

cook time
40 minutes

serves
8

plan ahead

Pizzetta squares may be prepared up to 2 weeks ahead and stored, well-wrapped, in the freezer.

These sophisticated flaky dough squares have a flavor reminiscent of pizza and are a snap to prepare.

- 2 tablespoons olive oil
- 4 medium onions, **cut into thin rounds**
- 1/3 cup sun-dried tomatoes, **finely chopped**
- 2 teaspoons mayonnaise
- 1 teaspoon dried oregano
- 2 frozen puff pastry sheets, **thawed**
- 3 teaspoons capers, **finely chopped**
- 10 fresh basil leaves, **finely chopped**

Prep: In a large skillet, heat oil over medium heat. Add onions and sauté until soft and golden, about 20 minutes. In a small bowl, combine tomatoes, mayonnaise and oregano.

Assemble: Preheat oven to 400°. Line 2 baking sheets with parchment paper. Lay pastry sheets on the parchment paper and pierce with a fork several times. Spread tomato mixture evenly over pastry sheets. Scatter onions on top. Top with capers and basil.

Bake: Bake uncovered for about 20 minutes or until pastry is puffed and golden. Let cool for at least 30 minutes. Cut into squares with a pizza cutter or sharp bread knife. Serve warm or at room temperature.

sausage skewers in creamy honey mustard sauce

prep time
15 minutes

cook time
6 minutes

serves
4

These mini skewers are a quick appetizer with big flavor. Use fresh, unwrinkled mini peppers for the best crunch.

- 4 fully-cooked Italian veal sausages or any flavored sausages, each cut into 6 pieces
- 24 mini bell peppers
- Salt and freshly ground black pepper, to taste
- ½ cup honey mustard
- 1 tablespoon soy sauce
- 1 tablespoon mayonnaise

special equipment
- 8 short bamboo skewers

Prep: Preheat broiler to low. Soak skewers in a pan of water for 15-20 minutes. Onto each skewer, thread 3 sausages with 1 pepper between each sausage piece onto each skewer and place on a baking sheet. Spray with cooking spray and season with salt and pepper. In a small bowl, whisk mustard, soy sauce and mayonnaise to blend.

Broil: Broil skewers until vegetables are lightly charred and crisp-tender and sausage is heated through. Turn occasionally and brush with mustard mixture during the last 1-2 minutes, about 6 minutes total.

Serve: Arrange skewers on a platter. Brush with remaining mustard sauce and serve.

17

foccacia with roasted salmon and summer vegetables

CONTRIBUTED BY AVI PIFKO, GRILLING EXPERT AND AFICIONADO

Grilling the foccacia dough gives each bite an unexpected smoky flavor. For the truly ambitious, try grilling the salmon for an added dimension of fresh summer taste.

- 1 ear of corn
- ½ pound salmon fillet
- 2 tablespoons plus ½ teaspoon extra-virgin olive oil
- Salt and freshly ground black pepper, to taste
- 1 bunch asparagus, trimmed and cleaned
- Purchased regular or whole wheat pizza dough, thawed
- ¼ cup purchased hummus
- One (8-ounce) jar roasted red peppers, cut into strips

Corn: Place corn in a small pot with water to cover. Bring to a boil and cook, covered, for 15 minutes. Drain and set aside. When cool, hold corn vertically and slice down, removing kernels.

Salmon: Preheat oven to 400°. Place salmon on a piece of foil and drizzle with ½ teaspoon olive oil. Season with salt and pepper and roast in oven until cooked through, about 16 minutes. When cool, flake salmon into large pieces.

Asparagus: In a medium pot, bring salted water to a boil. Place asparagus in water for 3 minutes or until they turn bright green. Remove and place in a bowl filled with ice water. Drain and set aside.

Pizza: Preheat grill to medium-high heat. Roll pizza dough to ⅛-inch thickness and drizzle with 1 tablespoon oil. Quickly and firmly flip dough onto grill, oiled side down, making sure to lay dough flat on grill. Baste top of dough with remaining 1 tablespoon oil and grill for 1-2 minutes or until bubbles begin to form on top and dough does not stick when lifted. Flip dough, close grill lid and grill for another 1-2 minutes, checking for doneness after 1 minute.

Toppings: Remove foccacia from grill and spread with hummus. Top with red peppers, corn, asparagus and salmon. Return it to grill on low heat for 1-2 minutes (or to preheated 300° oven for 5 minutes). Remove foccacia from grill or oven, slice and serve.

prep time
20 minutes

cook time
5 minutes
plus topping
cooking time

serves
6-8

simplify

Substitute frozen corn for fresh. Defrost and slice kernels off of cob.

cook's tip

Try different vegetables as toppings. String beans add a nice crunch and can substitute the asparagus when not in season.

prep time
40 minutes plus
chilling times

cook time
30 minutes

yields
18 calzones

plan ahead

Steak filling can be
made up to 1 day
ahead and stored,
tightly covered, in
the refrigerator.
Bring to room
temperature
before using.
Calzones can also
be prepared and
stored, uncooked,
for up to a day in
the refrigerator.
Glaze with egg
immediately
before cooking.

simplify

Substitute a
package of frozen
pie pastry dough (1
pound, 10 ounce),
thawed and mixed
with 2 teaspoons
paprika, for
homemade crust.
Beware – dough
must stay chilled or
it will not hold its
shape. Refrigerate
any unused dough
as you work, and
work quickly.

smoked rib eye calzones

A calzone is a small circle of dough folded in half, enclosing a filling. The flavors of the smoked rib eye are very sophisticated and delicious. This dish can be served as a beautiful appetizer with a drizzle of teriyaki or soy sauce over each calzone.

- 1 teaspoon paprika
- 1 teaspoon garlic powder
- 1 teaspoon sugar
- 1 teaspoon dried oregano
- 2 teaspoons chili powder
- 1½ teaspoons hickory smoke flavor*
- 1 (16-ounce) rib eye steak (about 1¼-inch thick)

- Salt and freshly ground black pepper, to taste
- 3 tablespoons olive oil
- 1 medium white onion (½ cup), chopped
- 1 large green bell pepper, chopped
- 3 tablespoons tomato paste
- 2 tablespoons fresh parsley, chopped
- Paprika Crust (*recipe to the right*)
- 2 eggs, beaten

Steak filling: Mix first 6 ingredients in a small bowl. Rub spice mixture all over both sides of steak. Refrigerate overnight.

Cook: Preheat a grill pan over medium-high heat. Season steak with salt and pepper. Grill for about 6 minutes per side for rare. Cool slightly. Trim and discard any fat and finely chop steak. Heat oil in a large nonstick skillet over medium-high heat. Add onion and bell pepper; sauté until tender, about 8 minutes. Add chopped steak and tomato paste; sauté for 3 minutes. Stir in parsley. Season with salt and pepper.

Fill dough: Line 2 large baking sheets with parchment paper. On a lightly floured surface, roll out a dough disk to a generous ⅛-inch thickness. Using a 4-inch-diameter plate or bowl as a guide, cut out rounds. Place 1 rounded tablespoon of steak filling on center of each dough round. Brush dough edges with egg. Fold dough over filling, covering filling. Using a fork, seal edges. Transfer to prepared sheets. Repeat with other dough disk and remaining filling. Gather and reroll dough scraps; cut out additional rounds until all dough is used.

Bake: Preheat oven to 375°. Brush calzones with remaining egg and bake until crust is golden, about 28 minutes. Transfer to plates.

*Hickory smoke flavor or liquid smoke offers a real hickory flavor without actually putting the food on the grill. It is sold in small bottles and available at most well-stocked grocery stores.

- 4 cups all-purpose flour
- 2 teaspoons paprika
- 1 teaspoon salt

- 1 cup (2 sticks) margarine, at room temperature
- ½ cup (or more) water, at room temperature

Blend flour, paprika and salt in a food processor fitted with an "S" blade. Add margarine by tablespoonfuls to food processor, pulsing until a coarse meal forms. Add ½ cup water; process until moist clumps form, adding more water by teaspoonfuls if dough is dry. Gather dough into a ball and divide in half. Flatten each half into a disk and wrap in plastic; let stand at room temperature for 30 minutes.

mini sweet potato latkes
with spiced apple cream

prep time
20 minutes

cook time
30 minutes

yields
48 latkes

The traditional potato latke has been kicked up a few notches with the addition of sweet potatoes, honey and spices. Topped with the sweet, spiced apple cream – it's almost a dessert!

- 2¼ pounds (3 large) red-skinned sweet potatoes, peeled
- 3 large eggs
- 6 tablespoons all-purpose flour
- ¼ cup honey
- 1 teaspoon ground cinnamon
- ½ teaspoon ground nutmeg
- ⅛ teaspoon cayenne pepper
- 1 teaspoon salt
- ¼ teaspoon ground black pepper
- Vegetable oil, for frying
- Spiced Apple Cream *(recipe below)*

Prep: Finely grate potatoes in a food processor. Press to remove all liquid and place in a large bowl. Add remaining ingredients, except oil, and mix well.

Fry: Coat bottom of a large skillet with oil and heat over medium heat. Drop batter, by tablespoonful, into the skillet. Press with a spatula to 1½-inch rounds. Fry until golden and cooked through, about 5 minutes per side. Transfer to paper towel-lined plates. Continue until batter is finished, draining off liquid that accumulates in batter and adding oil to the skillet as needed. Serve hot with Spiced Apple Cream.

spiced apple cream

- 1 medium apple (½ cup), peeled and finely diced
- 2 cups sour cream, at room temperature
- ¼ cup brown sugar
- ¾ teaspoon apple pie spice
- ⅛ teaspoon cayenne pepper
- Pinch of sea salt

In a medium bowl, combine all ingredients and mix well until smooth. Cover and refrigerate until ready to serve.

plan ahead
Mango Chutney can be made up to 4 days in advance and stored, covered, in the refrigerator.

tilapia sliders with mango chutney

Tiny sliders are the most popular finger food for a party or appetizer. Lightened up with tilapia and brightened with a crisp mango chutney, you will find this version irresistible.

- 1 pound tilapia fillets, skinned and cut into small chunks
- 1 tablespoon capers
- 1 medium red onion (½ cup), chopped
- 1 medium red pepper (1 cup), chopped
- ½ cup fresh parsley leaves
- 2 scallions
- 1 tablespoon Dijon mustard
- 1 cup mayonnaise
- 1 egg
- ½ cup panko bread crumbs

- 2 tablespoons olive oil
- 1 teaspoon kosher salt
- ½ teaspoon freshly ground black pepper
- ½ teaspoon herbes de Provence
- 1 teaspoon Old Bay Seasoning
- 4 radishes, sliced into rounds
- 1 bunch arugula
- Mango Chutney *(recipe below)*
- Super Quick Whole Wheat Slider Buns *(recipe on the right)*

Prep: In the bowl of a food processor fitted with an "S" blade, combine tilapia, capers, red onion, red pepper, parsley and scallions. Pulse 2-3 times, until pieces are uniform. Mix in mustard, mayonnaise, egg and panko bread crumbs. Refrigerate for 1 hour.

Cook: In a large skillet, heat oil over medium heat. Using slightly wet hands, form tilapia mixture into 1-inch balls about 1½ tablespoons in size. Place in the skillet and flatten using a spatula. Fry until golden brown, 2-3 minutes per side. Remove from the skillet and place on a large baking sheet. Bake at 400° for 8-10 minutes, until heated through.

Assemble: Cut slider buns in half. Spread 1 tablespoon of mango chutney on the bottom half. Layer 2 radish rounds, a few pieces of arugula, one tilapia patty and ½ tablespoon Mango Chutney. Top with other half of bun.

mango chutney

- ¼ cup fresh lemon juice
- ¾ cup vegetable oil
- ½ cup onions, chopped
- ½ cup scallions, chopped
- ¼ cup celery, chopped
- ½ cup unripe mango, finely chopped
- 4 cloves garlic, finely chopped
- 2 tablespoons prepared horseradish

- 3 tablespoons Creole or whole grain mustard
- 3 tablespoons yellow mustard
- 3 tablespoons ketchup
- 3 tablespoons parsley, chopped
- 1 teaspoon salt
- 1 teaspoon cayenne pepper
- ⅛ teaspoon freshly ground black pepper

Combine all ingredients in the bowl of a food processor fitted with an "S" blade and process for 30 seconds.

super quick whole wheat slider buns

These wholesome slider buns could not be easier to prepare. They are the perfect complement for meat or fish sliders and have an elegant presentation.

- 1 cup warm water
- 3 tablespoons warm water
- 2 tablespoons dry active yeast
- ¼ cup sugar
- 3½ cups whole wheat flour

- 1 teaspoon salt
- ½ teaspoon Herbs de Provence
- 2 eggs, **beaten, divided**
- ⅓ cup canola oil
- ⅓ cup quick cooking oats

Dough: Grease and flour 2 muffin tins. In a medium bowl, combine water, yeast and sugar. Let sit for 10 minutes or until bubbles form. In a separate bowl, combine flour, salt and Herbs de Provence. Add flour mixture to yeast and mix in 1 egg and oil. Let rest for 15 minutes. Roll into 18 balls and place in the prepared muffin tins. Brush buns with remaining egg and sprinkle with oats.

Bake: Bake at 400° for 8-10 minutes or until lightly browned. Be careful not to overbake or buns will be dry.

prep time
20 minutes

cook time
10 minutes

serves
10-12, 18 buns

cook's note

If you are baking in batches and have empty muffin spaces in your tin, fill halfway with water to prevent burning and ensure even baking.

chicken liver terrine
with olive tomato sauce

This is a beautiful centerpiece for a kiddush or formal lunch.

prep time
15 minutes

cook time
1 hour,
30 minutes

serves
8

- 4 ounces broiled chicken livers
- 3 cloves garlic, peeled
- 1½ cups soy milk, divided
- 5 large eggs
- ½ cup non-dairy tofu sour cream
- Salt and freshly ground black pepper, to taste
- 2 tablespoons finely chopped chives, plus more for garnishing
- Olive Tomato Sauce *(recipe below)*

Prep: Generously spray an oven-safe jello mold or deep, round pan with cooking spray. In a food processor fitted with an "S" blade, combine livers, garlic and 1 cup soy milk. Blend for about 1 minute until mixture is creamy. Add eggs, sour cream and remaining ½ cup soy milk. Season with salt and pepper. Blend for a few seconds to incorporate ingredients. This should yield 4 cups. Stir in chives and transfer to the prepared mold or pan.

Bake: Preheat oven to 375°. Place terrine in a roasting pan and fill the pan with warm water halfway up the sides of terrine. Bake for 1 hour, 15 minutes, or until completely set inside. A toothpick inserted in the center should come out clean. Allow to sit for 15-20 minutes.

Serve: To unmold terrine, gently run a knife around the warm mold or pan (if it has cooled, place in warm water for a few minutes), and sponge up any liquid that drains out of it. Pour Olive Tomato Sauce on top and around it, garnish with chives and serve immediately.

cook's note
When cooking with livers, cooked livers must be used. Raw livers must be kashered properly before being used.

This dish can also be prepared in a small loaf pan.

simplify
For Olive Tomato Sauce, use an undrained 32-ounce can of diced tomatoes to substitute for fresh tomatoes and tomato juice.

olive tomato sauce

- 1½ pounds (2 medium) tomatoes
- 1 large (1 cup) onion, chopped
- 8 ounces mushrooms, quartered
- 2 tablespoons olive oil
- 2 cloves garlic, chopped
- ½ cup tomato juice
- Salt and pepper, to taste
- 18 pitted green olives, finely chopped

Place tomatoes in a pot of boiling water for 10-15 seconds. Let cool for a few minutes. Peel, halve and press to remove seeds. Cut flesh into 1-inch pieces; this should yield 2½-3 cups. In a medium saucepan over medium heat, sauté onion and mushrooms in oil for 2-3 minutes. Add garlic and cook for 1 minute; add tomatoes, tomato juice, salt and pepper. Bring to a boil, and boil for 2-3 minutes. Stir in olives. Continue to boil for 1 more minute.

plan ahead

Dressing can be made up to 3 days ahead and stored, tightly covered, in the refrigerator.

spinach and marinated red pepper salad with couscous cakes

As the highlight of a salad, couscous takes on a new look. These crispy, crunchy cakes add just what you need to make this salad a beautiful vegetarian starter course for any meal.

- ¾ cup couscous
- 2 teaspoons kosher salt, divided
- 1 cup boiling water
- 1 large clove garlic, peeled
- ¼ cup packed fresh flat-leaf parsley leaves
- ½ cup canned chickpeas, drained and rinsed
- 2 large eggs, lightly beaten
- Finely grated zest of 1 medium lemon (about 1½ teaspoons)
- 3 tablespoons vegetable or canola oil, divided

- 8 ounces (about 6 lightly packed cups) baby spinach leaves, washed and dried
- ½ large red onion, sliced in semicircles
- 1 avocado, peeled, pitted and chopped
- 1 (8-ounce) jar marinated red pepper strips, cut into slices
- Creamy Dressing (*recipe to the right*)
- Kosher salt and freshly ground black pepper, to taste

garnish
- 8 fresh basil leaves, chopped

Couscous cakes: In a medium bowl, combine couscous and 1 teaspoon salt. Add boiling water and cover the bowl with a plate or pot lid. Let sit for 4-5 minutes. In a food processor fitted with an "S" blade, coarsely chop garlic. Add parsley and pulse until finely chopped. Add chickpeas and 1 teaspoon salt and pulse again until coarsely chopped. Uncover couscous and fluff with a fork. Stir in chickpea mixture, eggs and lemon zest until well combined. Press couscous into a ¼-cup measure, smooth top and invert the measuring cup to release the cake onto a plate. Repeat with remaining couscous to make 9 cakes.

Fry: Heat 1½ tablespoons oil in a large skillet over medium heat until shimmering hot. Add 5 couscous cakes to the skillet, using a spatula to lightly flatten the cakes so they are about ¾-inch thick. Fry, flipping once, until crisp and golden brown on both sides, 2-3 minutes per side. Transfer to a paper towel-lined plate. Add remaining oil to the skillet and fry remaining cakes.

Assemble: In a large bowl, toss spinach, red onion, avocado and red pepper strips with Creamy Dressing (you will have extra dressing). Season with salt and pepper. Divide among 3 individual plates and top each with 3 couscous cakes. Garnish with chopped basil leaves and drizzle with remaining dressing.

creamy dressing

- 2 tablespoons fresh lemon juice (from about 1 large lemon)
- 1 tablespoon mayonnaise
- 1 teaspoon fresh mint leaves, finely chopped
- 1 clove garlic, **minced**
- 1 teaspoon sugar
- 5 tablespoons extra-virgin olive oil
- Kosher salt and freshly ground black pepper, to taste

Combine lemon juice, mayonnaise, mint leaves, garlic and sugar in a small bowl. Slowly whisk in oil and mix well to combine. Season with salt and pepper.

stacked nori and sea bass

Nori is the Japanese name for dried seaweed. The finished product resembles a square of green paper. Nori has a delicious flavor and many nutritious qualities.

prep time
15 minutes

cook time
55 minutes

serves
8

plan ahead
Dressing can be prepared up to a week ahead and stored, covered, in the refrigerator.

- 1½ cups sushi or short grain rice
- 1¾ cups cold water
- 3 tablespoons rice vinegar
- 1 tablespoon sugar
- 1 teaspoon salt
- ½ pound Chilean sea bass fillet, skinned
- ¼ teaspoon black pepper
- ½ cup mirin (rice wine)
- 2 large seedless cucumbers, shredded or very thinly sliced
- 2 avocados, peeled, pitted and cubed
- 1 large carrot, peeled and shredded
- 2 nori sheets, crushed or cut into small squares
- Wasabi Soy Dressing (recipe below)

Rice: Rinse rice until water runs clear. Place rice in a medium saucepan with cold water and cook, covered, for 25 minutes. Turn off flame and let sit for 10 more minutes. In a small saucepan, combine vinegar, sugar and salt over low heat, stirring until sugar dissolves; do not let it boil. Pour over rice, using a wooden spoon to combine.

Sea bass: Preheat oven to 350°. Place sea bass in a roasting pan and season with pepper. Pour mirin over fish and bake, covered, for 30 minutes. Remove liquid and let cool. Flake fish with a fork and mix with half of Wasabi Soy Dressing.

Prepare stacks: Layer rice (shaping with your fingers or a shaped mold), cucumbers, avocados, carrot, sea bass and nori sheets. Pour dressing over layers and serve.

wasabi soy dressing

- 6 tablespoons low-sodium soy sauce
- 2 tablespoons mayonnaise
- 2 teaspoons wasabi powder

In a small bowl, combine all ingredients, mixing well to blend.

pineapple basil kani salad

Baby pineapple boats with a refreshing salad filling make this a beautiful starter course.

- 1 pound mock crab
- ½ teaspoon salt
- ¼ teaspoon freshly ground black pepper
- 2 firm-ripe baby pineapples with leaves, halved lengthwise
- ¼ cup peanut or vegetable oil
- 1 garlic clove, smashed
- 3 tablespoons pineapple juice

- 2 tablespoons fresh lime juice
- 1 tablespoon soy sauce
- 1 tablespoon sugar
- 1 small shallot, thinly sliced
- 1 red bell pepper, diced into ¼-inch pieces
- 3 tablespoons fresh mint leaves, chopped
- 2 tablespoons basil leaves, chopped

Prep: Season fish with salt and pepper. Using a grapefruit knife, remove fruit from pineapples in 1 or 2 large pieces, leaving the shells intact. Cut fruit into ½-inch pieces.

Cook: In a small saucepan over medium-low heat, cook oil and garlic, stirring until garlic is golden, about 2-3 minutes. Discard garlic. In a small bowl, combine garlic oil, pineapple juice, lime juice, soy sauce and sugar, whisking until sugar is dissolved. Add shallot, pepper, pineapple pieces and herbs. Toss fish with pineapple mixture and serve mounded in pineapple shells.

endive stuffed with fennel and ricotta

Each bite of salty cheese and crisp fennel will surprise you. The combination of flavors is outstanding!

prep time
5 minutes
serves
4

- 1 small fennel bulb, **trimmed, fronds reserved for garnish**
- ¼ cup shaved parmesan cheese
- ¼ cup ricotta cheese
- 1 tablespoon extra-virgin olive oil
- Salt and freshly ground black pepper, **to taste**
- 8 large endive leaves

garnish
- 4 radishes, **cut into matchsticks**

Prep: Cut fennel into quarters and discard core. Thinly slice enough fennel to measure ½ cup. Combine sliced fennel, parmesan cheese, ricotta cheese and oil in a small bowl. Add salt and pepper and toss to blend. Spoon equal amounts of fennel mixture into hollow side of each endive leaf. Garnish with fennel fronds and olives.

cook's note

Fennel has a very distinct taste. For those who prefer a different flavor, substitute with 2 teaspoons of a variety of fresh herbs, such as basil, thyme and oregano.

33

smoked salmon loaf

For a sure show-stopper, this smoked salmon loaf is a must. There is no baking involved and it tastes like a bagel with lox–perfect for a Sunday morning brunch.

- 3 (8-ounce) packages cream cheese, divided, softened
- 1 medium red onion (½ cup), finely chopped
- 2 tablespoons capers, drained and chopped
- 2 tablespoons fresh dill, finely chopped, plus more sprigs for garnish
- 1 teaspoon freshly squeezed lemon juice
- Salt and freshly ground black pepper, to taste
- 2 loaves pumpernickel bread, cut into 16 ½-inch slices, with crusts
- 1 pound smoked salmon, thinly sliced
- 1½ seedless cucumbers, thinly sliced into ⅛-inch slices, patted dry, plus more for decorating sides of loaf
- ½ cup crème fraiche or sour cream
- 2½ ounces salmon roe
- 1 ounce black caviar

garnish
- 2 lemons, cut in wedges

Prep: In a small bowl, combine 1 package cream cheese, red onion, capers, dill and lemon juice. Season with salt and pepper, and stir until smooth. Lay 4 bread slices on a clean work surface; trim about ¼ inch from all sides of each slice, creating even-size slices. Spread 2 tablespoons cream cheese mixture on 1 slice and layer with smoked salmon and cucumber (try not to overlap cucumber slices). Spread another thin layer of cream cheese mixture on top. Repeat with 2 remaining bread slices.

Stack: Neatly stack prepared slices, filling side up, squaring the sides with your hands; top with fourth bread slice. Repeat with remaining bread and filling to create three more stacks.

Decorate: Transfer stacks to a serving platter, arranging them very close together in a row. In a small bowl, combine remaining cream cheese and crème fraiche until smooth. Using an offset spatula, spread mixture evenly over assembled loaf. Refrigerate, covered with plastic wrap, for 2 hours or overnight. Before serving, arrange overlapping cucumber slices around base of loaf; spoon salmon roe and caviar along top of cake and sprinkle with dill. Garnish the platter with lemon wedges.

duck and wild rice salad
with orange shallot dressing

prep time
40 minutes
cook time
30 minutes
serves
6

For a truly outstanding beginning to your meal, serve this wild rice salad topped with crisp duck pieces and wait for the compliments to pour in. It is elegant enough for the most formal occasion, yet simple enough for anyone to prepare.

- 2 cups (10 ounces) wild rice
- 3 tablespoons olive oil
- 1 large onion (1 cup), finely chopped
- 4 cups water
- 3 cups chicken broth
- 2 (14-ounce) boneless duck breast halves with skin
- Salt and freshly ground black pepper, to taste
- 1 green pepper, diced

- 6 scallions, thinly sliced diagonally
- ¾ cup dried cranberries, chopped
- 1½ cups (4½ ounces) pecans, chopped and toasted
- 1 teaspoon salt
- Orange Shallot Dressing (*recipe below*)

garnish
- ⅓ cup French fried onions, crushed

plan ahead

Dressing can be prepared up to 2 days ahead and stored, covered, in refrigerator.

simplify

Use pre-cooked duck breasts.

Rice: Rinse rice well in a large sieve under cold water and drain. In a medium sauce pan, heat oil over medium heat. Sauté onion, stirring occasionally, until golden, about 5 minutes. Add rice and cook, stirring, until fragrant, about 3 minutes. Stir in water and broth and bring to a boil. Reduce heat and simmer, covered, until rice is tender, about 1-1¼ hours. (Grains will split open but not all liquid will be absorbed.) Drain well in a colander and cool.

Duck: Preheat oven to 375°. Pat duck breast halves dry and season with salt and pepper. Score skin in a crisscross pattern and place duck breast halves, skin sides up, in a lightly oiled shallow (1-inch-deep) baking pan. Roast in middle of oven until an instant-read thermometer inserted horizontally into center registers 120° (for medium-rare), about 25 minutes. Transfer duck breast halves to a cutting board, and when just cool enough to handle, remove skin. Cut duck breast halves in half horizontally (butterfly-style); then cut across the grain into thin slices.

Assemble: In a large bowl, combine rice, green pepper, scallions, dried cranberries, pecans and 1 teaspoon salt. Add dressing and toss gently. Using an ice cream scoop, place a mound of rice salad into martini glasses or onto individual serving plates. Arrange duck slices over rice and sprinkle with fried onions.

orange shallot dressing

- Zest of 1 orange, finely grated
- ⅔ cup fresh orange juice
- ⅓ cup extra-virgin olive oil
- ⅓ cup shallot, finely chopped

- 1 teaspoon fresh thyme, chopped
- 1 teaspoon brown sugar
- 1 teaspoon salt
- ½ teaspoon black pepper

Whisk together all ingredients in a large bowl and let stand at room temperature while making rice salad.

plan ahead

Dumplings can be refrigerated for up to 4 hours ahead.

soy dipping sauce

- 3 tablespoons soy sauce
- 1 tablespoon rice vinegar
- 1 teaspoon sugar
- ½ teaspoon sesame oil
- 1 scallion, thinly sliced

In a small bowl, combine soy sauce, vinegar and sugar. Mix until sugar is completely dissolved and then stir in oil and scallion.

chinese dumplings with veal and duck fillings

China has perfected the art of dumpling making over centuries. Here is a quick, authentic and delicious sampling of this Chinese delight.

- 1 (48-count) package 3x3-inch refrigerated wonton wrappers (e.g., Nasoya brand), defrosted
- Vegetable oil, if pan-frying

veal filling

- 2 cups green cabbage, finely chopped
- 2 teaspoons salt
- 12 ounces ground veal
- 3 medium scallions, thinly sliced
- 3 large cloves garlic, minced
- 2 tablespoons dry sherry
- 1½ tablespoons grated fresh ginger
- 1 tablespoon soy sauce
- 2 teaspoons toasted sesame oil
- ½ teaspoon sugar
- ¼ teaspoon freshly ground black pepper

duck filling

- ½ roast duck
- 8 dried shiitake mushrooms, soaked in hot water for 30 minutes
- 2 tablespoons water
- ½ teaspoon sugar
- 6 ounces spinach, washed and stems trimmed
- ¼ cup water chestnuts, finely chopped
- 2 medium scallions, thinly sliced
- 1½ tablespoons minced fresh ginger
- 1 tablespoon soy sauce
- 1 teaspoon cornstarch
- ¼ teaspoon freshly ground black pepper

Prep Veal: In a medium bowl, toss cabbage with salt and set aside for 30 minutes to shed moisture. Wring out cabbage in a clean dish towel to extract as much liquid as possible. In a large bowl, combine cabbage with remaining ingredients. Stir until well combined. Refrigerate for at least 20 minutes.

Prep Duck: Separate duck meat from bones and skin, and finely shred meat by hand. Place meat in a medium bowl. Cut stems from mushrooms and discard. Squeeze excess moisture from mushrooms, finely chop and add to duck. In a 12-inch skillet, bring water and sugar to a boil over high heat. Add spinach and cook, stirring until wilted, about 30 seconds to 1 minute. Squeeze excess water from spinach and transfer to a cutting board to cool. Finely chop. Stir spinach, water chestnuts, scallions, ginger, soy sauce, cornstarch and black pepper into duck and mushrooms. Let cool.

Fill and shape dumplings: Spoon 1-2 teaspoons of filling onto a wonton wrapper and brush edges with water. If boiling, fold wrapper in half and seal dumpling by pinching edges together. If pan-frying, fold sides in over and filling and pleat, pressing edges together, until wrapper forms a bundle. Press edges gently together to seal. This wide shape allows dumplings to sit upright in the pan and form a flat surface for browning. Repeat with remaining wrappers and filling. Arrange filled dumplings in a single layer on a large baking sheet without touching each other so they don't stick together.

If Boiling: Bring a large pot of salted water to a boil. Add dumplings, one at a time, making sure they don't stick together. Don't overcrowd the pot. Lower heat to medium and continue to boil, gently stirring occasionally, until they are cooked through, about 3-5 minutes. Remove and serve immediately with Soy Dipping Sauce.

If Pan-Frying: Heat 2 tablespoons oil in a 10- to 12-inch skillet over medium heat until shimmering hot. Arrange dumplings wide side down in concentric circles starting from the outer edge. Cook until golden brown on bottom, about 1-2 minutes. Pour in about ½ cup of water, enough to come about a third of the way up sides of dumplings. Bring to a boil, cover and cook until all water has been absorbed, about 7-10 minutes. Uncover, reduce heat and continue cooking until dumplings are dry and crisp on bottom, about 1-2 minutes. Invert the skillet onto a plate to flip dumplings and serve immediately with Soy Dipping Sauce.

soups

tuscan white bean, spinach and garlic soup

A piece of crusty bread on the side and you've got a meal-in-one –
a perfect lunch meal or hearty appetizer bound to satisfy a hungry soul!

- 2 cups dried White Cannellini or Great Northern beans
- 2 tablespoons olive oil
- 1 pound flanken, cut into large chunks (cut in between the bones)
- 2 shallots, chopped
- 5½ cups low-sodium chicken broth
- 1 cup water
- 4 cloves garlic, peeled and roughly chopped
- 1 teaspoon salt, plus more to taste
- ½ teaspoon freshly ground black pepper, plus more to taste
- 2 sage leaves, stems removed and thinly sliced
- 2 cups fresh baby spinach leaves

Soak: Place beans in a large bowl. Add enough water to cover by a few inches. Soak for at least 4 hours or overnight.

Sear: Heat oil in a large pot over high heat. Add flanken and brown on each side, about 1-2 minutes per side. Add shallots and cook until soft, stirring occasionally, about 2-3 minutes.

Simmer: Add broth, water, garlic, salt and pepper. Stir to blend and bring to a boil. Skim off any impurities that rise to the surface, if necessary. Cover and reduce heat to low, simmering until beans are fork-tender, about an hour.

Spinach: Add sage and spinach leaves right before serving and heat through for 5 minutes. Season to taste with more salt and pepper, if needed. Ladle soup into bowls, dividing portions of meat into each serving.

simplify
Substitute ½ cup frozen drained spinach for fresh.

plan ahead

Spiced Pumpkin
Seeds can be
made 3 days
ahead and stored
in a tightly sealed
container.

simplify

Purchased
seasoned croutons
can be substituted
as a garnish in
place of pumpkin
seeds.

chilled avocado gazpacho with spiced pumpkin seeds

Pumpkin seeds, or "pepitas" [puh-PEE-tahs] are a popular ingredient in Mexican cooking. Inside their white hulls are dark green seeds that have a deliciously delicate flavor—a great snack when roasted and salted, and a wonderfully crunchy accompaniment to this chilled soup.

- 2 tablespoons olive oil
- 1 white onion, sliced into rings
- 2½ cups low-sodium vegetable broth, or more as needed
- 3 medium ripe avocados, peeled, pitted and cut into large chunks
- ½ cup cilantro, chopped
- ¼ cup parsley, chopped
- 3 tablespoons fresh lime juice
- 1 teaspoon ground cumin
- 1 teaspoon ground coriander
- 1 teaspoon kosher salt, plus more to taste
- ½ cup sour cream or pareve tofu sour cream
- Freshly ground black pepper, to taste
- Spiced Pumpkin Seeds *(recipe below)*

Sauté: Heat oil in a medium skillet over medium-high heat. Add onion and sauté until translucent, about 6 minutes. Remove from heat and transfer to blender.

Pureé: Pureé sautéed onion together with broth, avocados, cilantro, parsley, lime juice, cumin, coriander and salt. Blend in the sour cream and season to taste with more salt and pepper. Refrigerate covered for at least 2 hours. Thin the soup with broth if necessary. Ladle into bowls and garnish with Spiced Pumpkin Seeds.

spiced pumpkin seeds

- 1 tablespoon olive oil
- ¾ cup raw green (hulled) pumpkin seeds
- ¾ teaspoon ground cumin
- Pinch of cayenne pepper
- Pinch of kosher or coarse sea salt

Heat oil in a small skillet over moderately high heat. Add pumpkin seeds and cook, stirring constantly, until seeds begin to pop, 1-2 minutes. Stir in cumin and cayenne pepper, and continue to cook, stirring until fragrant, about 30 seconds. Transfer to a bowl and season with a generous pinch of salt.

dilled tomato rice soup

Fresh herbs impart a vibrant flavor to this simple soup. When shopping, look for crisp herbs with a bright green color—avoid any with brown spots or soft areas. Fresh herbs are highly perishable and should be stored wrapped in a damp paper towel in your crisper to reduce spoilage.

prep time
10-15 minutes
cook time
50 minutes
serves
6

- 2 tablespoons olive oil
- 1 onion, diced
- 1 (15-ounce) can tomato sauce
- 2 tomatoes, diced
- 2 tablespoons onion soup mix
- 1 teaspoon curry powder
- 1 teaspoon sugar
- Kosher salt and freshly ground black pepper, to taste
- ¼ cup fresh dill, chopped, plus additional sprigs for garnish
- ½ cup uncooked white rice
- 6 cups water
- 6 basil leaves, chopped

simplify

Use a 15-ounce can of diced tomatoes in place of the fresh tomatoes, and substitute the fresh dill with 1 tablespoon dried dill.

Brown onions: Heat oil in a medium pot over medium-high heat. Add onion and sauté until onions begin to brown, about 15 minutes.

Simmer: Add all remaining ingredients, except basil leaves, and stir to blend. Bring to a boil and reduce heat to low. Cover and simmer for 20 minutes. Add basil leaves and simmer covered for an additional 10 minutes. Ladle soup into bowls and garnish with fresh dill sprigs.

Serving Option: Brown rice can be used instead of white rice. An additional 10 minutes of cooking time is required.

Dairy Serving Option: Place a dollop of sour cream in the middle of each individual bowl and top with dill.

prep time
20 minutes

cook time
8 hours,
30 minutes

serves
6

plan ahead

Beans can be
precooked up to 2
days in advance.
Store in a tightly
covered container
in the refrigerator.

cook's tip

To cook this soup
on the stove top,
precook beans as
directed above
for 45 minutes.
Rinse and drain,
then place all
ingredients (except
for spinach,
balsamic vinegar
and olive oil) in
a large stock pot
over medium-
high heat. Bring
to a boil, then
reduce heat and
simmer for 1½
hours, stirring
occasionally.
Add the spinach
and balsamic
vinegar in the last
five minutes of
cooking time.

triple "b" crock pot soup – beef, barley and beans

The rich, layered flavor produced by this soup belies its simple origins – slow-cooking in a crock pot.

- 1 cup dried multi-bean mix, picked over and rinsed
- 6 cups water
- 1 (14-ounce) can whole tomatoes with juice, broken into large pieces
- 3 cloves garlic, minced
- 2 ribs celery, chopped
- 2 medium carrots, chopped
- ½ medium onion, chopped
- ½ cup pearled barley
- 1 pound skirt steak, cut into chunks
- 1 bay leaf
- 1½ tablespoons kosher salt, plus more to taste
- 2 teaspoons dried Italian herb blend
- Freshly ground black pepper, to taste
- ½ ounce dried porcini mushrooms, about 1½ tablespoons
- 3 cups frozen spinach, thawed and drained
- 1½ tablespoons balsamic vinegar
- Extra-virgin olive oil

Precook beans: Place beans in a medium saucepan. Cover beans with water (enough to cover by 1-2 inches). Bring to a boil over medium-high heat, then lower to a simmer and cook covered for about 30 minutes (or until beans are firm, but tender enough to be pierced by a fork). Drain beans and rinse. Set aside.

Slow-cook: Place beans, water, tomatoes with juice, garlic, celery, carrots, onion, barley, skirt steak, bay leaf, salt, herb blend, pepper and mushrooms in a crock pot; cover and cook on low until the beans are quite tender and the soup is thick, about 8 hours.

Wilt spinach: Stir in the spinach and vinegar, cover and let the soup cook until the spinach wilts, about 5 minutes. If soup is too thick, adjust consistency by adding hot water by ¼ cupful and stir. Season to taste with salt and pepper. Drizzle each serving with olive oil.

spiced maple pumpkin soup
with sautéed cremini mushrooms

Chinese five-spice powder is a blend of the 5 most commonly used spices in Chinese cooking: star anise, cloves, cinnamon, fennel and black pepper. The blend is now currently available in many supermarkets, and adds a new dimension of flavor to this autumnal soup.

- 2 (15-ounce) cans pure pumpkin
- 4 cups water
- 1 cup half and half
- 1 garlic clove, crushed
- ¼ cup pure maple syrup
- 4 tablespoons unsalted butter, divided
- 2½ teaspoons Chinese five-spice powder
- 1½ pounds cremini mushrooms, thinly sliced
- Kosher salt and freshly ground black pepper, to taste

garnish
- Pita Chips *(recipe below)*

Simmer: Bring first 4 ingredients to a simmer in a large saucepan over medium-high heat, stirring often. Whisk in syrup, 2 tablespoons butter and five-spice powder. Continue to simmer for 10 minutes, whisking often. While soup simmers, prepare the mushrooms

Sauté: Melt remaining 2 tablespoons butter in heavy medium skillet over medium-high heat. Add mushrooms and sauté until tender, about 10 minutes. Remove from heat and season soup with salt and pepper. Divide among 6 bowls. Top soup with sautéed mushrooms and Pita Chips.

pita chips

- 2-3 pita breads, cut into strips
- Vegetable cooking spray
- ½ teaspoon cayenne
- ½ teaspoon cinnamon

Preheat oven to 400°. Prepare a baking sheet lined with foil. Arrange pita strip on the baking sheet. Spray with cooking spray. Dust with cayenne pepper and Bake for 2-3 minutes, or until golden.

simplify

Use whole peeled
roasted chestnuts,
available in sealed
pouches or jars

winter chestnut and parsnip bisque

Prepared chestnuts make this earthy soup a snap to prepare, lending a warm, nutty flavor. Serve with a chunk of crusty bread on the side—the perfect antidote for a cold winter's night.

- 2 tablespoons walnut or peanut oil
- 1 pound parsnips, peeled and cut into small chunks
- 2½ cups shelled roasted chestnuts, halved
- 1 medium onion, chopped
- 2 cloves garlic, minced
- ⅛ teaspoon white pepper
- ¾ teaspoon ground nutmeg
- ½ teaspoon ground ginger
- 5¼ cups (42 ounces) low-sodium chicken or vegetable broth
- 2 sprigs fresh marjoram
- 1 cup soy milk or cream, divided
- Kosher salt and freshly ground black pepper, to taste

garnish
- Snipped chives

Sauté: Heat oil in a large pot or Dutch Oven over medium-high heat. Add parsnips, chestnuts, onion, garlic and spices. Sauté for about 10 minutes or until parsnips are tender, stirring often. Add broth and bring to a boil. Reduce heat and simmer covered for about 20 minutes. Add marjoram; simmer for an additional 10 minutes. Remove marjoram and discard. Remove pot from heat and cool for 5-10 minutes.

Pureé: Using an immersion blender, pureé soup until smooth (this can also be done in batches in a food processor or blender).

Finish: Stir in ½ cup of soy milk or cream and season with salt and pepper. Ladle soup into bowls. Decoratively swirl 1 tablespoon of remaining soy milk or cream into each individual serving. Garnish with snipped chives.

chilled honeydew ginger soup

A great starter for a hot summer day, this elegant chilled soup is made simply in the food processor or blender. Look for a sweet, ripe melon to make your soup sing!

- 1 large ripe honeydew melon, peeled, seeded and cubed (approximately 8 cups)
- 1½ cups coconut milk
- ¼ cup honey, plus more to taste if the melon is not very sweet
- ¼ cup fresh lime juice
- 2 tablespoons freshly grated ginger
- Pinch of sea salt, plus more to taste

garnish
- chopped crystallized ginger, fresh mint leaves, sour cream

Blend: Place melon, coconut milk, honey, lime juice, ginger and a pinch of salt in the bowl of a food processor or blender. Process until the mixture is smooth, about 1-2 minutes. Season to taste with salt and additional honey if needed. Ladle soup into bowls and garnish with a dollop of sour cream sprinkled with chopped crystallized ginger and a mint leaf.

Serving Option: Soup can be served in small scooped out melon halves.

plan ahead
Soup can be made 2 days ahead and stored in a tightly sealed container in the refrigerator.

cook's tip
Freshly grated ginger keeps beautifully in the freezer so you can always have some on hand. Just remove the peel with the back of a metal spoon then grate finely with a microplane- no need to defrost!

honey roasted peach soup

When the weather is hot and peaches are at the height of the season, nothing beats this refreshing soup—a true summer delight! Freeze leftovers in popsicle molds for a cool frozen treat your family will love!

prep time
15 minutes

cook time
25 minutes

serves
8

- 6 large ripe peaches, peeled, halved and pitted
- 4 tablespoons brown sugar
- 3 tablespoons honey
- 2½ cups orange juice
- 1 teaspoon ground cardamom
- ½ teaspoon fine sea salt

- 1 teaspoon vanilla extract
- ½ teaspoon cinnamon
- Juice of one lemon, approximately 2 tablespoons

garnish
- Mint sprigs

plan ahead
Soup can be made 2 days ahead and stored in a tightly covered container in the refrigerator.

simplify
Use 2 cans of peaches in light syrup, drained, in place of the fresh peaches. Add ½ teaspoon nutmeg to the recipe.

Roast peaches: Preheat oven to 350°. Toss peaches with sugar and honey and lay on a parchment paper-lined baking sheet, cut side down. Roast for 15 minutes, turn over and roast 10 minutes more.

Blend: Scrape peaches and accumulated juices into the bowl of a food processor and blend until smooth. Add orange juice, cardamom, salt, vanilla extract and cinnamon. Blend until smooth. Transfer to a medium bowl. Season to taste with lemon juice. Cover and refrigerate for at least 2 hours. Serve chilled, garnished with a mint sprig.

Dairy Serving Option: For a richer, creamier soup, swirl ½ cup of crème fraiche or sour cream into the soup prior to serving.

plan ahead

Soup can be prepared 2 days in advance.
*If preparing in advance, skim off the layer of fat formed after the soup has been chilled.

simplify

For garnish, Terra chips stix make a good substitute in place of the tortilla strips.

mexican meatball soup with tortilla strips

Inspired by the traditional Spanish and Mexican meatball soup, "Sopa de Albondigas," this hearty soup is a flavorful meal-in-one.

meatballs
- 1½ pounds lean ground beef
- ½ cup coarsely grated zucchini (about ½ medium unpeeled zucchini)
- ½ cup finely chopped onion
- ½ cup panko bread crumbs
- 1 large egg, **beaten**
- 2 teaspoons dried oregano
- 1½ teaspoons kosher salt

soup
- 1 tablespoon olive oil
- ¼ cup finely chopped onion
- 2 cloves garlic, **minced**
- 6 cups beef stock
- 4 cups water
- 1 teaspoon dried oregano
- 1 cup coarsely grated zucchini (about 1 medium unpeeled zucchini)
- Kosher salt and freshly ground black pepper, to taste

garnish
- ¼ cup fresh cilantro, **chopped**
- Tortilla Strips *(recipe below)*

Meatballs: Place all meatball ingredients in a large bowl and gently mix together until combined. Using slightly wet hands, shape into 1-inch meatballs. Set aside.

Soup: Heat oil in a large pot or Dutch Oven over medium heat. Add onion and garlic, and sauté until translucent, about 4-5 minutes. Add beef stock, water, and oregano and bring to a boil. Reduce heat to low and simmer covered for 10 minutes. Add zucchini, stirring to blend. Carefully drop in meatballs. Bring soup back to a simmer, adjusting heat as necessary. Cover and cook meatballs over low heat, stirring occasionally, until cooked through (about 25-30 minutes). Skim excess fat off surface of soup, if necessary.* Season with salt and pepper. Ladle soup with meatballs into bowls and top with chopped cilantro and Tortilla Strips.

tortilla strips

- 6 tablespoons vegetable oil
- 8 corn tortillas, cut into ¼-inch-wide strips

Heat 3 tablespoons oil in a large skillet over medium heat. Add half of tortilla strips and gently separate with tongs or a wooden spoon. Fry until lightly golden in color. Transfer strips to paper towels to drain. Repeat with remaining oil and strips.

caramelized butternut squash and pear soup

All the fragrant tastes of autumn are represented here in one great soup!
Make this soup in the fall when pears and winter squash are at the height of the season.

prep time
30 minutes

cook time
1 hour,
30 minutes

serves
8-10

- 1 large butternut squash (about 3 pounds), peeled, seeded and cut into 1-inch pieces
- 2 carrots, peeled and cut into 1-inch pieces
- 2 tablespoons extra-virgin olive oil
- Kosher salt and freshly ground black pepper, to taste
- 3 leeks, white and light green parts only, cleaned and sliced
- 3 Bosc pears, peeled, cored and cut into 1-inch pieces
- ½ cup white wine
- ¼ cup brandy
- 3 tablespoons apple juice concentrate, thawed if frozen
- 6 cups low-sodium chicken or vegetable broth
- 2 cups water
- 7 tablespoons honey
- 1 large fresh thyme sprig, plus additional leaves for garnish
- 1-inch piece fresh ginger, peeled and grated

garnish
- 1 tablespoon chopped crystallized ginger

Roast vegetables: Preheat oven to 450°. Arrange squash and carrots in a single layer in a large roasting pan. Drizzle with oil, and season with salt and pepper. Roast for 10 minutes, and then add leeks and pears. Toss to combine and continue to roast for another 30 minutes, or until tender and golden brown.

Simmer stock: Remove pan from oven. Add wine, brandy and apple juice concentrate, using a wooden spoon to scrape up the vegetables and their caramelized juices from the sides and bottom of the pan. Transfer vegetables and liquid to a large stock pot. Add broth and water, adding additional water if necessary to cover the vegetables by 1 inch. Add honey, thyme sprig and grated ginger and bring liquid to a boil. Reduce the heat and simmer, partially covered, for about 45 minutes or until vegetables are soft and tender when pierced with a fork.

Pureé: Remove thyme sprig and pureé soup with an immersion blender, or in batches in a blender or food processor. Add a small amount of water to thin slightly. Season to taste with salt and pepper. Ladle soup into bowls and garnish with crystallized ginger and a sprinkling of fresh thyme leaves.

simplify

Purchase ready-made packaged butternut squash soup. Combine with 3 jars pureéd pear baby food and 4 jars pureéd carrot baby food in a soup pot. Bring to a simmer and mix in brandy, wine, leeks, honey, thyme and ginger. Season with salt and pepper. Bring to a boil, then lower to a simmer. Cover and cook for approximately 45 minutes over low heat. Proceed with the directions above for pureéing the soup.

prep time
30 minutes
approximately

cook time
1 hour

serves
6

cream of roasted red pepper soup

Roasted red peppers are usually used as an accompaniment to a main dish—as the focal point of this soup, the caramelized flavor is pronounced and delicious!

- 4 red bell peppers, cut in half and seeded
- 2 tablespoons olive oil
- Kosher salt, to taste
- 1 large onion, diced
- 1 (28-ounce) can plum tomatoes, drained
- 1 cup dry red wine
- 1 cup tomato juice
- 2 sprigs fresh marjoram
- 3 cups low-sodium vegetable broth
- 1½ teaspoons sugar
- Freshly ground black pepper, to taste
- 1 cup heavy cream

garnish
- ¼ cup sour cream
- ¼ cup fresh basil leaves, chopped

Roast peppers: Place oven rack about 3-4 inches from the top of the oven. Preheat oven to 500°. Place pepper halves on a foil-lined baking sheet, cut side up. Brush the inside of peppers with olive oil and sprinkle with salt. Turn pepper halves over (skin side up) and roast until skin is charred and blistering, about 15 minutes. Remove from oven, cover with foil, and cool for at least 10 minutes. Remove foil and carefully peel away the peppers' skin from the flesh. Discard skins and finely chop the peppers.

Blend: In a blender, pureé tomatoes and peppers. Set aside.

Sauté: Heat oil in large saucepan over medium heat. Add onion and sauté until translucent, about 5-6 minutes. Add blended peppers and tomatoes, wine, tomato juice, marjoram, broth, sugar, salt and pepper. Bring to a boil. Reduce heat and simmer for 20 minutes, stirring occasionally. Remove marjoram and discard. Stir in heavy cream and season with salt and pepper. Remove from heat. Ladle soup into bowls, top with a dollop of sour cream and a sprinkling of chopped basil.

Serving Option: Soy milk and tofu sour cream can be substituted for dairy ingredients to make a pareve soup.

homey chicken fricassee

This is a real old country dish, perfect for cold Sukkos nights. Fricassee is great to do ahead, as the flavors will intensify the longer it sits.

prep time
25 minutes

cook time
2 hours,
40 minutes

serves
8-10

- 4 tablespoons olive oil
- 2 cups finely chopped onion, divided (about 2 medium onions)
- 2 stalks of celery, chopped
- 1½ pounds chicken drummettes
- 1-1¼ pounds chicken giblets
- 2 pounds chicken wings, cleaned and pinfeathers removed
- 1-1½ pounds chicken necks
- 2 pounds lean ground beef
- 1 egg, beaten
- ¼ cup matzo meal
- 3 teaspoons salt, divided
- 2 teaspoons paprika
- Freshly ground black pepper, to taste

Sauté: In a large pot, heat oil over medium heat. Add 1½ cups chopped onion and celery, and sauté until translucent and soft, about 10-15 minutes. Add drummettes, chicken giblets, wings and necks into the pot. Fill with enough water to cover. Bring to a boil and skim off any impurities that rise to the surface. While the soup is boiling, prepare the meatballs.

Meatballs: In a large bowl, combine ground beef, remaining ½ cup chopped onion, egg and matzo meal. With slightly wet hands, form small meatballs and carefully drop them into the soup. Add 1 teaspoon salt and paprika.

Simmer: Bring the fricassee to a boil and reduce heat to low. Cover and simmer for two hours. Season with 2 teaspoons salt and pepper to taste.

plan ahead

Fricassee can be made up to 4 days in advance. Meatballs can be mixed and formed a day ahead, and refrigerated until cooking time. This recipe also freezes beautifully. Simply bring to room temperature after cooking, transfer to freezer-safe containers and cover tightly. Always leave a little room for ice expansion when freezing liquids.

prep time
20 minutes

cook time
45 minutes plus
chilling time

serves
8

plan ahead

Coconut soup
can be made in
advance and
freezes beautifully.
Pineapple rounds
can be made a day
ahead and stored
in the refrigerator.

simplify

Use canned
pineapple rings
in place of fresh.
Decrease the
pineapple juice
added while
roasting to a total
of 4 tablespoons.

chilled tropical coconut soup with roasted pineapple

Roasted pineapple is a vibrant, sweet addition to this summer soup – perfect as a starter or even as a dessert.

- 4 cups canned unsweetened coconut milk
- 1½ cups unsweetened shredded coconut
- 1 cup sugar, divided
- 24 whole cloves, divided
- 1 (4½-pound) fresh pineapple, peeled, cored and sliced into ½-inch rounds
- 1 vanilla bean, split lengthwise or 1 teaspoon vanilla extract
- 6 tablespoons pineapple juice

Boil: Bring coconut milk, shredded coconut, ½ cup sugar and 8 cloves to a simmer in a large heavy saucepan, whisking until sugar dissolves. Remove from heat, cover and set aside to cool. Strain coconut soup through a fine sieve set over a large bowl, pressing on solids to extract as much liquid as possible. Refrigerate until cold, at least 2 hours.

Roast pineapples: Preheat oven to 375°. Place pineapple slices on a large rimmed baking sheet (you may need a second pan). Stud each piece with remaining cloves and set aside. Place remaining ½ cup sugar in a small bowl. Using the tip of a sharp knife, carefully scrape the seeds from the vanilla bean into the sugar. Mix to blend. Sprinkle vanilla sugar over pineapple. Place pineapple slices in the oven and roast for 15 minutes. Drizzle 3-4 tablespoons of pineapple juice over sliced pineapple to prevent burning. Roast for another 15 minutes and repeat with remaining juice. Finish roasting for additional 15 minutes. Pineapple is done when slices are tender and pan juices are a syrupy, golden brown. Remove from oven and cool pineapple completely. Let stand at room temperature.

Serve: Ladle soup into 8 bowls. Top each bowl with a pineapple round. Drizzle with pan juices.

salads

summer salad
with sweet poppy seed dressing

Summer is the season for cool, crisp salads- hearty enough to satisfy, light enough to refresh. Tropically inspired, this salad just seems to fit the bill.

prep time
15 minutes

cook time
6-7 minutes

serves
8

plan ahead
If not serving immediately, rewarm mushrooms prior to serving.

- 2 tablespoons olive oil
- ½ pound assorted mushrooms (e.g., shiitake and button), stems removed and sliced
- 1 head red leaf lettuce, torn into bite-size pieces
- 1 head green leaf lettuce, torn into bite-size pieces
- 1 medium red onion, cut into thin rounds (optional)
- 1 avocado, cut into chunks
- 1 ripe mango, cut into bite-size chunks
- 1 red bell pepper, chopped
- 1 yellow pepper, chopped
- 1 green pepper, chopped
- 1 (16-ounce) can hearts of palm, sliced into thick rounds
- ⅓ cup craisins
- Sweet Poppy Seed Dressing *(recipe below)*
- ⅓ cup toasted almonds

Sauté: In a medium skillet, heat oil over medium heat and sauté mushrooms for 6-7 minutes or until soft.

Mix: In a large bowl, combine lettuces, onion, avocado, mango, peppers, hearts of palm, craisins and mushrooms. Add dressing and toss to combine. Sprinkle almonds on top and serve.

sweet poppy seed dressing

- ½ small onion
- 1 teaspoon salt
- 1 teaspoon dry mustard
- 4 tablespoons cider vinegar
- ½ cup sugar
- ½ cup oil
- 1 teaspoon poppy seeds

Blend all dressing ingredients in a food processor with "S" blade or use an immersion hand blender.

kani cucumber cole slaw

prep time
15 minutes
serves
6

plan ahead

Dressing may be
prepared up to
a week ahead.

simplify

Use purchased
spicy mayonnaise
and combine
with 2 teaspoons
sesame oil.

Using a mandolin or Japanese slicer makes short work of this Asian-style slaw. Kani is Japanese for "crab"; kosher mock-crab sticks can be found in the freezer section of the supermarket and shred effortlessly once defrosted.

spicy mayonnaise dressing
- ½ cup mayonnaise
- ½ teaspoon cayenne pepper
- 2 teaspoons sesame oil
- 1 teaspoon honey

- 1 long seedless cucumber, halved and cut into long, thin ribbons with a mandolin or slicer
- 10 kani sticks, cut into long, thin ribbons or shredded
- 1 small red onion, cut into thin rings
- 3 tablespoons cilantro, chopped

Prep Dressing: In a small bowl, combine dressing ingredients and mix well.

Assemble: In a large bowl, combine cucumber, kani, onion and cilantro. Pour dressing over vegetables and mix to combine well. Serve immediately.

Every cook needs a go-to backyard barbecue salad that can be relied upon for cook-outs. Look no further - these vibrant colors of summer's bounty are a treat to behold both for the eyes and the palate.

cook time
30 minutes
serves
8

- 12 ears fresh corn
- 1 packet Italian dressing mix
- ⅓ cup olive oil
- ⅓ cup red wine vinegar

- 3 red bell peppers, **cut into 2-inch pieces**
- 1 cup black olives, pitted and sliced
- 1 (12-ounce) jar roasted red peppers, **drained and sliced if necessary**

plan ahead

Salad can be prepared a day ahead and stored, covered, in the refrigerator.

Corn: In a large stock pot, place corn in salted water to cover. Bring to a boil. Reduce to low and continue to cook for 20 minutes. Drain and let cool. Holding corn vertically, with a sharp knife, slice corn off the cob in a downward motion. Repeat with each ear of corn. Place corn in a large bowl.

Prep Dressing: In a cruet or small bowl, combine dressing powder, oil and vinegar. Shake or mix well to combine.

Assemble: In a large mixing bowl, combine corn, peppers, olives and jarred red peppers. Pour dressing over vegetables and toss to combine.

mom's pastries' warm mushroom salad with salmon

CONTRIBUTED BY MOM'S PASTRIES OF CEDARHURST, NEW YORK

Mom's Pastries has provided us with the recipe to their outstanding warm mushroom salad so you can recreate their delicious salad at home any time!

- 2 tablespoons olive oil
- 2 cups button mushrooms, sliced
- Balsamic Glaze (recipe below)
- ½ pint cherry tomatoes, halved
- 15 roasted almonds
- 1 (8-ounce) salmon fillet, cut into chunks
- 6 cups romaine pieces

Prep: In a medium skillet, warm 1 teaspoon olive oil over medium heat. Sauté mushrooms until soft and add balsamic glaze, tomatoes and almonds. Continue cooking for 5 minutes, until slightly reduced.

Salmon: In a separate medium skillet, warm remaining olive oil over medium heat. Place salmon pieces in the pan and cook 2-3 minutes per side, until crispy.

Assemble: In a large bowl, combine tomato/almond mixture and romaine. Add in salmon and toss to combine.

Serving Option: This salad makes a beautiful appetizer. Plate the salad components on individual plates and arrange salmon pieces on top. Drizzle any leftover glaze over salmon.
This recipe serves 4 as an appetizer.

prep time
3 minutes

cook time
5-7 minutes

serves
2 as a main dish
4 as an appetizer

cook's note

Balsamic glaze will solidify if left to cool. Rewarm in a microwave on low or over a low flame.

balsamic glaze

- ⅓ cup balsamic vinegar
- 2 teaspoons mustard
- 2 teaspoons honey

Place all ingredients in a small saucepan over medium heat. Bring to a boil and cook for 10 minutes on high, watching closely for burning, until reduced to a glaze.

crunchy rice salad
with soy sauce garlic dressing

Warm rice salads are simple to prepare and can be served at virtually any kind of meal. If preparing in advance, be sure to bring to room temperature prior to serving.

- ¾ cups uncooked white rice
- 1 cup pine nuts, toasted
- 1 cup mushrooms, sliced
- ½ cup bean sprouts
- ½ cup craisins
- 2-4 shallots, chopped
- ½ cup thin chow mein noodles
- 1 tablespoon fresh parsley, chopped
- Soy Sauce Garlic Dressing *(recipe below)*

Prep: Prepare rice according to package instructions. Drain and let cool.

Assemble: In a large bowl, combine pine nuts, mushrooms, bean sprouts, craisins and shallots. Add rice and mix gently. Before serving, add chow mein noodles, sprinkle with parsley and drizzle dressing on top.

soy sauce garlic dressing

- ½ cup oil
- ¼ cup soy sauce
- 2 cloves garlic, minced

In a small bowl, combine dressing ingredients and mix well.

watermelon salad with sugared pecans and blue cheese

The combination of watermelon with blue cheese may seem strange at first – but with one bite, the salty-sweet contrasts will be immediately understood...and loved!

prep time
15 minutes

cook time
10 minutes

serves
8

- 1 tablespoon butter
- 2 tablespoons dark brown sugar
- ¾ cup pecan halves, coarsely chopped
- 6-8 cups mixed baby greens or arugula, roughly chopped
- Raspberry Vinaigrette *(recipe below)*
- 2½-3 pounds watermelon, quartered lengthwise and cut crosswise into ¾-inch-thick cubes
- ½ cup blue cheese, crumbled
- ½ small red onion, halved and thinly sliced

Candy pecans: Melt butter in a heavy medium nonstick skillet over medium heat. Add sugar and stir to blend. Add nuts and stir to coat. (Butter may separate.) Transfer to a plate and cool. Store in an airtight container at room temperature.

Assemble: Place greens in a large bowl with vinaigrette to coat, reserving a few tablespoons vinaigrette. Divide salad among individual plates. Gently place watermelon cubes on each plate and sprinkle with cheese, red onion and sugared nuts. Drizzle with remaining vinaigrette.

cook's tip
Gorgonzola cheese or feta cheese are great options as blue cheese substitutions.

simplify
Substitute purchased honey-glazed pecans for the sugared pecans. Use purchased raspberry vinaigrette—add 2 tablespoons balsamic vinegar and mix well.

raspberry vinaigrette

- ¼ cup seedless raspberry jam
- ¼ cup cranberry juice
- 2 tablespoons balsamic vinegar
- 2 tablespoons white wine vinegar
- 6 tablespoons extra-virgin olive oil
- Kosher salt and freshly ground black pepper, to taste

Pureé jam, juice and vinegars in a blender until smooth. With machine running, gradually add oil. Season with salt and pepper. Store in an airtight container in the refrigerator.

dried fruit salad with balsamic dressing

This is a great winter salad, perfect to rely upon when seasonal fruits are sparse and the roads are snowy. Dried fruits have a long shelf-life and will stay for months.

- 6 cups mesclun greens
- 10 strawberries, thinly sliced
- ½ cup dried mango, chopped
- ½ cup dried blueberries
- ¼ cup craisins
- 1 medium red onion, diced
- 8 ounces glazed pecans, crushed
- Balsamic Dressing *(recipe below)*

Assemble: In a medium-size bowl, combine all ingredients except dressing and gently toss. Add dressing right before serving.

Serving Option: To serve individually, mound a scoop of greens and onion on individual plates or in martini glasses. Sprinkle remaining ingredients over greens and drizzle with dressing.

balsamic dressing

- 1 packet Italian dressing mix
- ½ cup balsamic vinegar
- ¼ cup sugar
- ½ cup olive oil

In a cruet or zip top bag, combine all ingredients and mix thoroughly.

...mber salad with red onion

...rsion of the classic pickled cucumber salad. Simple, straightforward, delicious.

...ing

...inegar

...se

...dill, chopped

- 8 Kirby cucumbers,
  peeled and sliced into 1-inch rounds
- ½ medium red onion,
  cut into thin rounds and halved
- 4 scallions,
  thinly sliced (green parts only)

Prep Dressing: In a small bowl, combine all ingredients. Whisk together until emulsified.

Assemble: In a medium bowl, combine cucumbers, red onion and scallions. Toss gently to combine. Pour dressing over vegetables. Combine well and serve.

Ripe, garden-fresh tomatoes require almost no effort in order to showcase their true flavor. Their deep, earthy sweetness shines right through with just a small amount of extra-virgin olive oil and fresh basil leaves.

- 3 large ripe tomatoes, **halved and sliced ½-inch thick**
- ½ teaspoon kosher salt
- ¼ teaspoon freshly ground black pepper
- 2 tablespoons extra-virgin olive oil

- 1 tablespoon balsamic vinegar
- 2 teaspoons fresh orange juice
- 8 large fresh basil leaves, **cut into a chiffonade**

Assemble: Place sliced tomatoes in a bowl. Sprinkle with salt and pepper. In a small bowl, combine oil, vinegar and orange juice. Pour over tomatoes. Toss gently to combine. Add basil leaves and serve.

Serving Option: Substitute basil leaves with a few tablespoons of chopped mint leaves for a crisp, fresh taste.

3-5 minutes

serves

4

cook's note

A chiffonade is the process of cutting herbs by stacking the leaves, rolling them tightly and cutting across with a sharp knife.

81

salmon salad with creamy dill dressing

Salmon salads are incredibly versatile – they serve beautifully as an appetizer, salad course or entrée. Our version incorporates green peas and craisins, lending a sweet, fresh flavor to this dish.

- 2 (8-ounce) salmon fillets
- 1 head romaine lettuce, sliced into thin ribbons
- 1 pint grape tomatoes, halved
- 2 cucumbers, peeled and sliced
- 1 cup frozen green peas, defrosted
- ⅓ cup craisins
- 1 medium red onion, sliced into rings
- ½ cup salad croutons
- Creamy Dill Dressing *(recipe below)*

Prep: Preheat oven to 400˚. Spray a baking pan with cooking spray and bake salmon fillets, covered, for 20 minutes. Once salmon has cooled, use a fork to gently flake into pieces.

Assemble: In a large bowl, place romaine, tomatoes, cucumbers, peas, craisins and onion. Pour dressing over salad and toss to combine. Sprinkle with croutons and serve.

creamy dill dressing

- 3 cloves garlic, crushed
- 1 cup mayonnaise
- ¼ cup tarragon vinegar
- ¼ cup sugar
- ¼ cup water
- ¼ cup fresh dill

In a salad cruet or zip top bag, combine ingredients and shake or mix until well combined.

spinach with goat cheese, roasted beets and pears

When a local eatery suddenly closed its doors, we had unresolved cravings for their special signature salad. Here is our recreation of Bari's goat cheese and beet salad, a neighborhood favorite.

prep time
20 minutes
cook time
1 hour,
50 minutes
serves
6

- 1 bunch beets (3 medium-size beets), red or orange
- Goat cheese log (6-7 ounces)
- 1 egg
- 1 teaspoon water
- 1½ cups panko bread crumbs
- 2 tablespoons olive oil
- 4 cups baby spinach leaves
- 1 cup arugula
- ½ cup walnut pieces, toasted
- 2 ripe pears such as Bartlett or D'Anjou, peeled and sliced into 12 pieces each
- Raspberry Vinaigrette *(recipe below)*

Prep: Preheat oven to 350°. Remove and discard beet greens. Wash beets very well, leaving peel on. Wrap in heavy duty foil and place on a baking sheet. Bake in oven for 1½ hours. Remove and let cool. With your fingertips, rub the outside of beets to easily remove skin. Slice beets into rounds and then into matchstick-size strips. Set aside.

Goat cheese rounds *(not featured in photo)*: Slice goat cheese log into 12 equal round slices. In a shallow plate, beat egg with teaspoon of water. Pour panko bread crumbs into a separate shallow plate. Dip cheese into egg and then dredge in panko bread crumbs, covering both sides. Repeat for all 12 slices.

Fry: Heat oil in a large skillet over medium heat. Place 6 goat cheese rounds in oil. Fry about 3 minutes per side, until golden brown. Place on a paper towel-lined plate. Repeat with next 6 slices.

Mix: In a large bowl, toss spinach leaves, arugula, walnuts and pears with raspberry vinaigrette. Add beets immediately prior to serving (beet juice will discolor and stain pears).

Serve: On 6 small plates, place a mound of salad blend and top with 2 goat cheese rounds. Serve immediately.

cook's tip

To create raspberry vinegar, soak 1 teabag of raspberry zinger tea in ½ cup white vinegar at room temperature for 4-6 hours. You may also substitute with balsamic vinegar.

plan ahead

Vegetables can be prepped a day ahead.

raspberry vinaigrette

- ½ cup raspberry vinegar
- ½ cup sugar
- 2 teaspoons Dijon mustard
- ¼ teaspoon dried oregano
- ½ cup vegetable oil
- Salt and pepper, to taste

Place vinegar, sugar, mustard and oregano in the bowl of a blender or food processor and purée until smooth. Slowly add oil until well combined. Season with salt and pepper.

plan ahead
This recipe can
be made 4 hours
ahead. Put in
covered container
and refrigerate.
Add peanuts
immediately
before serving.

sweet potato salad
with ginger and peanuts

Sweet potatoes and brown sugar are a classic combination. Transformed into a salad, with crispy, crunchy textures, the pairing is taken to new heights.

- ¼ cup white wine vinegar
- ¼ cup soy sauce
- 3 tablespoons mayonnaise
- 4 teaspoons fresh ginger, peeled and minced
- 4 teaspoons toasted sesame oil
- 5 cloves garlic, minced
- 1 tablespoon peanut butter
- 2 teaspoons chili sauce
- 1½ teaspoons dark brown sugar
- 2 pounds red-skinned sweet potatoes (yams), peeled and cut into ½-inch cubes
- 1½ cups sugar snap peas, cut crosswise into ½-inch pieces
- 1 cup scallions, thinly sliced
- 2 cups green cabbage, thinly shredded
- Kosher salt and freshly ground black pepper, to taste
- ⅓ cup dry-roasted peanuts, coarsely chopped

Prep Dressing: In a medium bowl, whisk vinegar, soy sauce, mayonnaise, ginger, sesame oil, garlic cloves, peanut butter, chili sauce and brown sugar to blend.

Cook: Place sweet potatoes in a large saucepan and add water to cover. Cook until tender, about 18 minutes. Drain in a large colander and rinse with cold water to halt cooking process. Let cool.

Combine: Mix sweet potatoes, dressing, peas, scallions and cabbage in a large bowl. Season with salt and pepper. Sprinkle salad with peanuts and serve.

grapefruit salad
with candied pecans and avocado

Vivid color contrasts make this one of the more decorative salad choices. Filled with antioxidants, it is also one of the healthiest as well - dig in!

plan ahead

Dressing can be prepared a day ahead and stored, covered, in the refrigerator.

walnut shallot dressing
- 1 shallot, **minced**
- 3 tablespoons reserved grapefruit juice
- 3 tablespoons champagne vinegar
- 3 tablespoons sugar
- ⅓ cup roasted walnut oil
- Kosher salt and freshly ground black pepper, **to taste**

- 4 cups romaine, **chopped**
- 4 cups baby spinach leaves
- ½ cup honey-glazed pecans
- 1 avocado, **diced**
- 1 red grapefruit, **peeled and segmented (reserve juice)**
- 1 small red onion, **thinly sliced**

Prep Dressing: In a small bowl, combine first four dressing ingredients. Whisk in oil to combine. Season with salt and pepper

Assemble: In a large bowl, combine all salad ingredients. Toss with Walnut Shallot Dressing and serve.

pomegranate jicama salad

Jicama (pronounced Hee-ka-ma) is a root vegetable with a mild, sweet, crunchy flavor. Here it is paired with tropical mango and pomegranate, with a splash of apple cider vinegar.

prep time
15 minutes
serves
6

apple cider vinaigrette
- ¼ cup apple cider vinegar
- 1 teaspoon salt
- ¼ cup pomegranate juice
- 1 tablespoon Dijon mustard
- ½ cup sugar
- ½ medium red onion
- ¼ cup olive oil

- 1 head romaine lettuce, cut into bite-size pieces
- 1 cup pomegranate seeds
- 1 medium-size jicama, peeled and cubed
- 1 avocado, cubed
- 1 mango, cubed

cook's note

To seed a pomegranate, cut in ¼s and place in a bowl filled with cold water. Pry seeds out while in water; seeds will fall to bottom of bowl and the white pith will float.

Prep Dressing: Place all ingredients into a food processor and pulse or blend until emulsified.

Assemble: In a medium bowl, combine lettuce, pomegranate seeds, jicama, avocado and mango. Pour dressing over salad and serve.

peppers with feta, cucumber and green apple

prep time
10-15 minutes
serves
8

Feta cheese lends a salty contrast to this sweet, crispy salad!

- ¼ cup sherry wine vinegar
- ¼ cup extra-virgin olive oil
- 2 tablespoons thinly sliced mint leaves
- 1 tablespoon chopped fresh oregano
- Fine sea salt and freshly ground black pepper, to taste
- 1 small red bell pepper, halved, seeded and cut into thin strips
- 1 small yellow bell pepper, halved, seeded and cut into thin strips
- 1 small green bell pepper, halved, seeded and cut into thin strips
- 1 small red onion, halved lengthwise and thinly sliced crosswise
- 1 cup English hothouse cucumber, cut into matchstick-size strips
- 4 plum tomatoes, halved, seeded and cut lengthwise into thin strips
- 1 (8-ounce) Granny Smith apple, cored and cut into matchstick-size strips
- 8 ounces feta cheese, crumbled

Dressing: In a small bowl, whisk vinegar and olive oil to blend. Stir in mint and oregano. Season dressing with sea salt and pepper.

Assemble: In a large bowl, toss peppers, onion, cucumber, tomatoes and apple. Add dressing and toss to coat. Season with sea salt and pepper. Sprinkle with feta cheese and serve.

seared tuna salad
with raspberry vinaigrette

The bright tartness and subtle sweetness of raspberry breathes new life into this crisp spinach and fresh tuna salad.

- 2 (1-1½ inch thick) tuna steaks
- Salt and freshly ground pepper, to taste
- 8 cups baby spinach
- 1 small red onion, diced
- 2 avocados, pitted, and cut into long, thin slices
- ¾ cup walnuts or pecans, toasted and roughly chopped
- Raspberry Vinaigrette *(recipe below)*

Prep: Season tuna with salt and pepper on both sides. Spray a grill pan with cooking spray.

Grill: Heat a grill pan over medium-high heat. Sear tuna for 1-1½ minutes on each side, leaving a browned edge on both sides of tuna with the center remaining pink. Let cool. With a very sharp knife, slice against the grain into thin slices.

Assemble: In a large bowl, combine baby spinach, onion and avocados with dressing. Toss to combine. Arrange tuna and walnuts or pecans over salad and serve.

raspberry vinaigrette

- ¼ cup raspberry jam
- ½ cup olive oil
- 3 tablespoons raspberry vinegar (see page 85 for tip)
- 3 tablespoons honey

In a small sauce pan over low heat, melt raspberry jam. Remove from fire and cool slightly. Add remaining ingredients and mix well.

herbed flower salad

This salad is beautiful as an appetizer for a Shavous meal. Your table will look like a freshly grown flower garden!

prep time
10-15 minutes
serves
6

- 1 cup mayonnaise
- ½ cup reduced-fat sour cream
- ½ cup chopped scallion (green part only)
- 2 tablespoons fresh thyme, chopped
- 2 tablespoons capers, chopped
- 4 anchovy fillets packed in oil, drained
- 2 tablespoons fresh lemon juice
- Kosher salt and freshly ground black pepper, to taste
- 4 heads assorted lettuce (e.g., red leaf, red leaf, Boston and Bibb), leaves separated and left whole

Blend: Pulse together mayonnaise, sour cream, scallion, thyme, capers, anchovy fillets and lemon juice in a food processor until smooth and pale green. Season with salt and pepper. Keep in covered container in refrigerator until ready to serve.

Assemble: In 6 clear individual bowls, arrange lettuce leaves in circles, one circle for each color of lettuce you are using: Arrange red leaf lettuce in a complete circle around the bowl's edge. Then layer the Boston leaves inside the red leaf lettuce and end with the Bibb leaves, the yellow cluster at the center. Drizzle salad dressing on top and serve.

Serving Option: This may also be made in one large bowl and served as a large salad. Simply use the same layout of lettuce leaves, but use all of the lettuce for each layer.

fish

halibut with peanuts and honey mustard glaze

Halibut is a firm-fleshed fish, yet mild in taste. Bold ingredients and contrasting textures help to accentuate its "personality," as achieved in the recipe below.

prep time
20 minutes

cook time
12 minutes

serves
6

- ⅓ cup seasoned rice vinegar
- 8 tablespoons vegetable oil, divided
- ½ cup honey mustard
- 2 tablespoons soy sauce
- ¾ pound fresh shiitake mushrooms, stems discarded and caps cut into ¼-inch-thick slices
- ½ cup roasted salted peanuts, coarsely chopped
- Salt and pepper, to taste
- 6 pieces halibut fillet with skin (2 pounds)

garnish
- 2 tablespoons chopped parsley

Prep Glaze: In a small bowl, whisk vinegar, 7 tablespoons oil, honey mustard and soy sauce until well combined; transfer ¾ cup glaze to another bowl.

Cook: Heat remaining oil in a large skillet over medium-high heat until hot but not smoking. Add mushrooms and sauté, stirring, until golden brown and crispy, about 6 minutes; transfer to a bowl and toss with peanuts. Season with salt and pepper.

Broil: Preheat broiler to medium. Lightly oil a baking pan. Rinse halibut and pat dry. Arrange, skin side down, on prepared pan. Spread ¾ cup glaze over halibut and broil 4 inches from heat until golden brown and just cooked through, about 10 minutes. If halibut browns too quickly, lower rack and continue to broil. Using 2 large spatulas, transfer halibut to a serving platter, top with mushroom mixture and garnish with parsley. Serve with remaining glaze on the side.

prep time
15 minutes plus
marinating time

cook time
8 minutes

serves
4

plan ahead
Blueberry salsa
may be made a
day ahead and
stored, covered, in
the refrigerator.

simplify
Use purchased
Italian dressing.

salmon skewers
with fresh blueberry salsa

CONTRIBUTED BY AVI PIFKO, GRILLING EXPERT AND AFICIONADO

Grilling salmon infuses the fish with a unique smokiness unlike any other cooking method. Paired with the fresh blueberry salsa, this dish can be used as a refreshing appetizer or light entrée.

- 12 ounces salmon fillet, skinned and cubed
- Italian Dressing *(recipe below)*
- Blueberry Salsa *(recipe below)*
- Long wooden skewers, soaked in water for 20 minutes

Prep: Thread salmon cubes onto skewers and place in a shallow dish. Pour Italian dressing over salmon and marinate for 30 minutes. Transfer dressing into a small saucepan and bring to a boil. Reduce heat to low and simmer for 5 minutes. Set aside.

Grill: Preheat grill to medium-high and grill salmon skewers for about 4 minutes per side, brushing frequently with reserved Italian dressing, until fish flakes easily with a fork. Serve with blueberry salsa.

italian dressing

- 6 tablespoons olive oil
- 2 tablespoons white wine vinegar
- 2 tablespoons fresh chopped parsley
- 1 tablespoon fresh lemon juice
- 2 cloves garlic, chopped
- 1 teaspoon dried basil
- ½ teaspoon dried oregano

In a small bowl, whisk together olive oil, vinegar, parsley, lemon juice, garlic, basil and oregano until well combined.

blueberry salsa

- 1 cup fresh blueberries
- 2 Persian cucumbers, chopped
- ½ small red onion, chopped
- 1 tablespoon extra-virgin olive oil
- Splash of lime juice
- Salt and pepper, to taste

In a bowl, place ingredients and toss to combine.

ginger glazed tuna

Wasabi is a green Japanese horseradish root with a strong, potent flavor. Tempered with a sweet ginger marmalade, the wasabi paste adds a slight kick to these tuna steaks.

- 2 tablespoons soy sauce, **divided**
- 4 (6-ounce) tuna steaks (1-inch thick)
- 1½ teaspoons sea salt
- 2 tablespoons ginger marmalade (e.g., Dundee)
- 2 teaspoons wasabi paste

Prep: Spoon 1 tablespoon soy sauce over tuna steaks; let stand for 5 minutes. Season with sea salt. In a small bowl, combine remaining soy sauce, ginger marmalade and wasabi paste, whisking to blend.

Grill: Heat a grill pan over medium-high heat. Coat pan with cooking spray. Add tuna to pan and cook for 2-3 minutes on each side. Spoon marmalade mixture over tuna; cook for 1 more minute or until medium-rare. Remove tuna from pan and serve.

braided salmon

The unique presentation of this salmon makes for a stunning centerpiece dish. Minimal effort, outstanding results!

- 2 teaspoons fresh ginger, **finely chopped**
- ½ teaspoon salt
- ½ teaspoon peanut oil
- ½ cup chives, **chopped**
- 2 teaspoons low-sodium soy sauce
- 1 teaspoon dark sesame oil
- 1 (1½-pound) skinless salmon fillet (preferably from the tail)

Prep: In a small bowl, combine ginger, salt and peanut oil. Brush over fillet and set aside. In a separate bowl, combine chives, soy sauce and sesame oil.

Braid: Preheat oven to 350°. Cut salmon vertically into 3 (15x1-inch) ropes; reserve remaining salmon for another use. Braid ropes and secure with toothpicks. Place braid in an 11x7-inch baking dish. Cover and bake for 22-25 minutes. Remove from oven, uncover and let stand for 10 minutes. Drizzle chive mixture over fish.

prep time
5 minutes

cook time
22-25 minutes

serves
6

cook's note

If you don't have a salmon tail or your salmon is very thick, slice the top off of the salmon to create a more even piece that is easier to braid.

tilapia with pistachio crust and mango salsa

Mango salsa is delicious all on its own, but yields especially delectable results when cooked with Tilapia. A pistachio crunch finishes this oven-fried fish with a nicely browned crust.

prep time
10 minutes
cook time
10 minutes
serves
4

plan ahead
Salsa can be made a day ahead and stored covered, separately, in the refrigerator.

- 1 cup shelled raw unsalted pistachios, toasted and finely chopped
- 1 cup panko bread crumbs
- Kosher salt and freshly ground black pepper, to taste
- 4 (7 to-8-ounce) tilapia fillets
- Mango Salsa *(recipe below)*
- 3 tablespoons canola oil, divided

Prep: Preheat oven to 425°. Spray rimmed baking sheet with cooking spray. In a small bowl, combine pistachios and panko bread crumbs. Season with salt and pepper. Spread 1 tablespoon puréed salsa over top of each fillet. Press pistachio mixture onto purée.

Cook: Heat 2 tablespoons of oil in a large nonstick skillet over high heat. Place fish in skillet, crust side up. Drizzle with remaining canola oil. Cook for 2 minutes and transfer to prepared baking sheet. Bake fish in oven until opaque in center, about 8 minutes. Serve with whole Mango Salsa on the side.

mango salsa

- ½ cup fresh mango, chopped (1 mango)
- ⅓ cup red pepper, chopped (1 medium-size red pepper)
- 5 scallions, chopped (green part only)
- ¼ cup water
- ⅛ teaspoon chili powder
- 2 tablespoons orange liqueur

Mix all salsa ingredients together in a medium bowl. Let sit for at least 30 minutes. Transfer half of mixture to a food processor and process together until smooth. Set aside.

salt encrusted bronzino

A salt crust locks in moisture and adds tenderness to the whole bronzino.

prep time
10 minutes

cook time
30 minutes plus
10 minutes
resting time

serves
4

- 3 egg whites
- ½ cup water
- 6 cups kosher salt
- 2 tablespoons coriander seeds
- 1 teaspoon fennel seeds
- 1 tablespoon whole black peppercorns
- 2 pounds cleaned whole bronzino, fins and scales removed
- 1 cup leek, thinly sliced (white and pale green parts only)
- 1 shallot, thinly sliced
- 1 clove garlic, thinly sliced
- 1 lemon, thinly sliced into rounds

  garnish
- 1 lemon, cut into wedges
- Extra-virgin olive oil

Prep: Preheat oven to 450°. Place rack in center of oven. Line large baking/cookie sheet (about the same size as fish) with foil, leaving a generous overhang. In a large bowl, whisk egg whites and water until blended. Add kosher salt and stir until evenly moistened.

Toast: In a small skillet, over medium heat, combine coriander, fennel and peppercorns. Toast for 9 minutes, stirring frequently, until popping begins. Remove from heat and coarsely crush with the back of a skillet or a mallet.

Stuff: Rinse fish inside and out and pat dry. Fill fish with leeks, shallots, garlic and lemon slices. Sprinkle with toasted crushed spices.

Seal: Pour 2 cups salt mixture onto the foil-lined sheet. Place fish on salt and cover completely with remaining salt mixture so no fish is showing. Use additional salt if necessary. Press to seal.

Bake: Bake fish for 25 minutes uncovered. Remove from oven and let rest in crust for 10 minutes. Using a large knife, rap on crust to crack it. (This is not a delicate dish–use force when cracking.) Brush salt from fish and cut into portions. Serve with lemon wedges and a drizzle of extra-virgin olive oil.

lemon flounder with shiitake crust

Get ready for a fried fish makeover. A shiitake mushroom crust trumps the typical batter hands-down for a taste that is anything but ordinary.

prep time
10 minutes
cook time
10 minutes
serves
4

- 6 tablespoons olive oil, divided
- 3 large shallots, chopped (½ cup)
- ¼ cup dry white wine
- ¾ cup soy milk or cream
- 4 tablespoons margarine or butter, cut into ½-inch cubes
- 2 teaspoons fresh lemon juice
- Kosher salt and freshly ground pepper, to taste
- ½ ounce package dried shiitake mushrooms
- ¾ teaspoon salt
- 4 (6-ounce) flounder fillets

Prep: Preheat oven to 350°. In a medium skillet, heat 2 tablespoons oil over medium heat. Add shallots and sauté until soft, about 2 minutes. Add wine and cook until most liquid evaporates, about 2 minutes. Add soy milk or cream and simmer until sauce thickens slightly, whisking occasionally, about 4 minutes. Add cold margarine or butter to sauce, a few cubes at a time, whisking until incorporated before adding more. Whisk in lemon juice and season with salt and pepper. Remove from heat. Cover sauce to keep warm while cooking fish.

Mushrooms: Sprinkle fillets with salt and pepper. Place dried mushrooms in a blender and grind to a fine powder. Transfer to a plate and mix in ¾ teaspoon salt. Press fillets into mushroom powder to coat on all sides.

Sauté: Heat remaining 4 tablespoons oil in a large ovenproof skillet over medium-high heat. Add fish to skillet and sauté until golden brown on bottom, about 3 minutes. Using 2 large spatulas, carefully turn over fillets. Transfer to oven and cook until fillets are just opaque in center, about 7 minutes. Place fillets on individual plates, drizzle with sauce and serve.

salmon on wine-soaked plank

Deep, smoky cedar scents seep into the salmon while grilling, lending it an incomparable flavor. Salmon can be presented on the plank..."oven to table" serving in a whole new light!

prep time
10 minutes
plus plank-
soaking time

cook time
30 minutes

serves
8

cook's note

Cedar planks can be purchased in some grocery stores and may be soaked in a variety of liquids. If you have nothing on hand, water may be used.

- 1 cedar plank, soaked for 1-4 hours in wine or beer
- 2 tablespoons sea salt
- 1 side of salmon
- 2 onions, sliced into rounds
- 1 zucchini, unpeeled, sliced into rounds
- 1 red pepper, cut into long, thin strips
- 6-8 baby portabella mushrooms, quartered
- 2 tablespoons olive oil
- Salt and freshly ground black pepper, to taste
- 1 teaspoon garlic powder
- ½ teaspoon paprika

Prep: Preheat grill to medium. Season the plank with sea salt and rub in to bring out the flavor. Rinse salmon and dry with paper towel. Place salmon on the plank and surround with vegetables. Brush fish and vegetables with olive oil and season with salt, pepper, garlic powder and paprika.

Grill: Place plank in center of grill and close the cover. Grill for approximately 30 minutes. Remove from grill and let rest for 5 minutes. Serve fresh.

beer battered cod

Traditional "fish 'n chips" have long used beer in the batter to create a light and crisp crust with a superior, robust flavor.

prep time
5-10 minutes

cook time
30 minutes

serves
6

- Canola or peanut oil
- 3 cups all-purpose flour, divided
- 1½ teaspoons salt, plus more for seasoning
- ¾ teaspoon freshly ground black pepper, plus more for seasoning
- 2 cups beer
- 3 eggs, beaten
- 3 pounds cod or tilapia fillets, cut into 3-inch pieces

Prep: Fill a deep-fryer or stock pot halfway with oil. Heat oil over medium heat until hot and beginning to bubble. In a large bowl, combine 2 cups of flour, salt, pepper and beer. Let stand for 10 minutes. Add eggs and mix to combine. Batter should be thin. Season fish with salt and pepper. Place 1 cup remaining flour in a large, shallow plate. Coat fish in flour, shaking off excess, and then dip in batter to coat.

Fry: Fry fish in batches until golden brown on both sides, about 10-12 minutes. Remove with a slotted spoon and set on a paper towel-lined plate.

Serving Option: Serve with purchased tartar sauce mixed with 1½ teaspoons hot sauce.

cook's note

Fish is best served fresh, but can be reheated, uncovered, in a 300° oven for 10 minutes.

prep time
15 minutes plus
marinating time

cook time
10 minutes

serves
4

mango-margarita flounder

A margarita is a drink made of tequila, orange-flavored liqueur and a citrus juice. We use these bright flavors with the addition of mango to create a delicious accent for flounder.

- 4 (6-ounce) flounder fillets
- 3 tablespoons tequila
- ½ cup orange liqueur (such as Cointreau)
- ¼ cup mango juice
- ¾ cup fresh lime juice (from about 9 limes)
- 1 teaspoon salt
- 3 large cloves garlic, peeled
- 4 tablespoons olive oil, divided
- 3 medium plum tomatoes, diced
- 1 mango, diced
- 1 medium red onion, chopped
- 1 small jalapeño, seeded and minced
- 3 tablespoons chopped fresh cilantro
- 1 tablespoon honey
- Salt and freshly ground black pepper, to taste

Prep: Place fish in a shallow baking dish. In a medium bowl, stir together tequila, orange liqueur, mango juice, lime juice, 1 teaspoon salt, garlic and 2 tablespoons oil. Pour mixture over fillets and rub into fish. Cover and refrigerate for 30 minutes, turning fillets once. In a medium bowl, toss together tomatoes, mango, red onion, jalapeño, cilantro and honey. Season with salt. Set salsa aside. Remove fillets from marinade and pat dry. Brush fillets with remaining oil and sprinkle with pepper. In a small saucepan, boil marinade for several minutes until slightly thickened. Remove from heat and strain out garlic cloves. Set aside to cool.

Grill: Preheat grill or a grill pan to high, or set oven to broil. Grill fish for 5 minutes on each side or until fish flakes easily with a fork. Transfer fish to a serving dish.

Serve: Serve with a spoonful of salsa and drizzle with reserved marinade.

broiled red snapper
with sweet pickle tartar sauce

Tartar sauce is a creamy condiment classically used with fish. Our version incorporates sweet pickles for a tangy twist.

prep time
5 minutes

cook time
6 minutes

serves
6

- ¼ cup mixed sweet pickles, finely chopped
- 4 teaspoons Dijon mustard
- ¼ cup mayonnaise
- 1 teaspoon pickle juice
- ½ teaspoon salt, divided
- ¼ teaspoon black pepper, divided
- 4 tablespoons extra-virgin olive oil
- 6 (4 to 6-ounce) pieces red snapper fillet with skin

garnish
- Lemon wedges

Prep: Preheat broiler to low. Place oven rack 5-6 inches from heat. Spray a shallow baking pan with cooking spray.

Sauce: In a small bowl, combine pickles, mustard, mayonnaise, pickle juice, ¼ teaspoon salt and ⅛ teaspoon pepper.

Broil: Arrange fish, skin sides down, in baking pan and sprinkle with remaining ¼ teaspoon salt and remaining ⅛ teaspoon pepper. Brush oil on fish and broil until fish is just cooked through, 4-6 minutes. Serve with 1 tablespoon sweet pickle tartar sauce spread on each piece of fish, garnished with lemon wedges.

chilean sea bass packets with garlic-clementine confit

Baking fish in parchment paper is known as en papillote. It infuses the fish with maximum flavor and minimum fuss.

- 4 (6-ounce) Chilean sea bass fillets
- 1 clementine
- Extra-virgin olive oil, for drizzling
- Salt and freshly ground black pepper, to taste
- Garlic-Clementine Confit *(recipe below)*

Prep: Preheat oven to 350°. Using a vegetable peeler, remove clementine peel in 4 2-inch-long strips. Cut parchment paper into 4 12-inch squares and center sea bass fillets onto each one. Drizzle fish lightly with oil and season with salt and pepper. Place 1 clementine peel strip, cut side up, on each fillet. Bring both edges of the parchment paper together underneath fillet to create a packet. Place parchment packets onto a rimmed baking sheet.

Bake: Bake fish in oven just until cooked through, about 22 minutes (fish is done when it easily flakes with a fork).

Serve: Remove fish from oven and unwrap fish. Place fillets onto individual plates, spoon confit over fillets and serve.

garlic-clementine confit

- 3 clementines
- ⅓ cup fresh Italian parsley, chopped
- 2 cloves garlic, peeled and minced
- 1 teaspoon salt
- ¼ cup extra-virgin olive oil

Using a vegetable peeler, remove peel (orange part only) of clementines. Chop peel (reserve flesh for another use). In a small bowl, combine peel, parsley, garlic and salt. Stir in oil and set mixture aside.

poultry

caramelized onion
chicken breast sandwiches

There is little comparable to the burst of flavor achieved when caramelizing onions—transforming an ordinary sandwich to extraordinary. A quick and easy recipe to prepare, dinner will be on the table as soon as the onions are cooked.

prep time
10 minutes
cook time
40-45 minutes
serves
6

- 2 tablespoons vegetable oil
- 2 pounds sweet onions (such as Vidalia), sliced into thin rings (about 7 cups)
- Salt and freshly ground black pepper, to taste
- 1½ pounds skinless, boneless chicken breasts, trimmed, pounded thin and halved
- 6 sourdough sandwich rolls, cut in half
- 3 cups baby arugula
- Extra-virgin olive oil, for brushing chicken and rolls
- Zesty Paprika Mayonnaise *(recipe below)*

Caramelize the onions: Heat vegetable oil in a large skillet over medium-high heat. Add onions and sauté until golden brown, stirring frequently, about 30 minutes. Season to taste with salt and pepper. Remove from heat. Set aside.

Prepare the chicken: Preheat oven to 475°, or alternatively, preheat your grill pan. Brush chicken breast with olive oil and sprinkle chicken with salt and pepper. Broil or cook in pan until cooked through, about 4 minutes per side. Remove from heat.

Assembly: Brush cut side of rolls with olive oil. Place rolls on grill pan or in oven broiler for 3 minutes, until grill marks appear or golden brown. Spread rolls with Zesty Paprika Mayonnaise, then layer the chicken, onions and arugula.

Serving Option: To use as an appetizer or party food, prepare these sandwiches on crusty, grained bread. Slice into long thin sandwiches with a big serrated knife.

plan ahead

Spread can be made 2 days in advance. Cover prepared spread and chill. The extra spread can be added to salad dressings or can be used instead of mayonnaise.

simplify

Use leftover cooked chicken, preferably chicken breast. 2 frozen garlic cubes can be substituted for fresh; defrost first.

zesty paprika mayonnaise

- ½ cup low fat mayonnaise
- 1 tablespoon fresh lime juice
- 1 teaspoon smoked paprika
- 2 cloves garlic, peeled and crushed

- 1½ tablespoons extra-virgin olive oil, plus more for brushing on rolls
- Kosher salt and freshly ground black pepper, to taste

Mix together mayonnaise, lime juice, paprika and garlic in small bowl. Whisk in olive oil. Season to taste with salt and pepper. Set aside.

prep time
10-15 minutes plus marinating time

cook time
40-50 minutes

serves
8-10

plan ahead
This recipe freezes beautifully. Reheat uncovered to crisp the skin.

simplify
12 frozen garlic cubes can be substituted for fresh.

whole broiled chicken
with lemon garlic marinade

Though seemingly simple, the bright fresh flavors of this chicken will surprise you.

- 2 whole or quartered chickens, rinsed and patted dry
- Kosher salt and freshly ground black pepper, to taste
- ⅓ cup olive oil
- ½ cup freshly squeezed lemon juice
- 10-12 cloves garlic, minced
- 2 tablespoons parsley, chopped

Marinate: Season the chicken with salt and pepper. Combine oil, lemon juice, garlic and parsley in a large ovenproof baking dish. Whisk to blend. Place seasoned chicken in mixture, and turn to coat. Marinate for 2–3 hours, turning several times. Drain off half of the marinade.

Broil: Preheat broiler. Broil chicken for 40 minutes, turning chicken every 10 minutes. A whole chicken (or very large pieces) may require 50 minutes of broiling time, or until well browned.

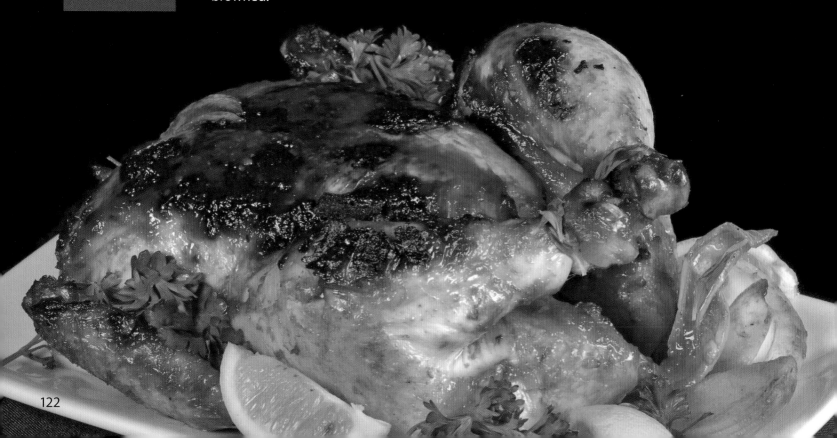

orange glazed chicken italiano

The most concentrated flavor in an orange is hidden in its peel. It is for this reason that orange marmalade provides such a terrific orange taste in this easy-to-prepare dish.

- 8 chicken thighs, bone-in with skin
- Kosher salt and freshly ground black pepper, **to taste**
- 1 (12-ounce) jar orange marmalade
- 2 packets Italian dressing powder

- 2 tablespoons olive oil
- ¼ cup apple cider vinegar
- ¼ cup ketchup

garnish
- Sesame seeds

prep time
10 minutes

cook time
2 hours

serves
4-6

plan ahead
Marmalade mixture can be made a day ahead and stored in a container in the refrigerator.

Prep: Preheat oven to 350°.

Dress Chicken: Place chicken pieces in a 9" x 13" baking pan. Sprinkle with salt and pepper. Mix the rest of the ingredients together in a small bowl. Spread mixture evenly over chicken pieces.

Bake: Bake 1 hour uncovered. Turn chicken pieces over and baste with sauce. Bake for 25 minutes, then turn back over and bake for an additional 25 minutes. Chicken should look browned and glazed. Sprinkle sesame seeds over baked chicken, and serve.

fresh herb butter

- ½ cup margarine or butter substitute, room temperature
- Juice and zest of 1 large lemon
- 1½ tablespoons parsley, **chopped**
- 1½ teaspoons dried tarragon
- 1½ teaspoons chives, **minced**

In a small bowl, cream the margarine and add the remaining ingredients. Transfer mixture to a large piece of parchment or waxed paper, and then, using the paper, mold into a thick square. Wrap well in the paper. Cover and refrigerate until firm.

panko-crusted chicken breasts
with fresh herb infusion

Often white meat gets dried out during the cooking process. A hidden pat of herbed "butter" adds an extra boost of moisture to the chicken, plus an infusion of flavor!

- ⅓ cup flour
- ½ teaspoon kosher salt
- Freshly ground black pepper, to taste
- 3 eggs
- 2 tablespoons water
- 6 skinless, boneless chicken breasts, cut in half
- Oil for frying
- 1 cup panko bread crumbs
- 1½ teaspoons dried parsley flakes
- Fresh Herb "Butter" *(recipe to the left)*

Prepare Fresh Herb "Butter."

Set up: Combine the flour with salt and pepper in a shallow bowl. In a separate bowl, beat the eggs together with 2 tablespoons water. Place the bread crumbs and parsley on a plate. Set aside.

Assembly: Lay the chicken cutlets out on a flat surface. Make a slit in the thicker side of each piece, forming a small pocket; do not cut all the way through the cutlet. Cut the "butter" into 6 pieces and insert one into each pocket. Press the edges of the pocket together so that the "butter" is not visible. Dredge each chicken cutlet first in the flour, then in the egg and last in the bread crumbs. Cover the coated pieces and refrigerate for a few hours.

Fry: Heat a layer of oil in a large frying pan over medium heat (about ½ inch covering the bottom of the pan). When oil is hot, fry the cutlets until golden brown, turning once halfway through, about 3-4 minutes per side. Using a slotted spatula or tongs, transfer to a paper towel-lined plate to drain.

prep time
30 minutes

cook time
15-20 minutes
plus 30 minutes
chilling time

serves
6-8

plan ahead

Fresh Herb "Butter" can be prepared up to 1 week in advance and stored wrapped in the refrigerator.

simplify

No time to fry? Oven fry! Lay breaded chicken breasts on a greased foil-lined cookie sheet and drizzle with 2 tablespoons oil. Bake in preheated 375° oven for 10-15 minutes, depending on thickness. Turn cutlets over, drizzle with additional 2 tablespoons oil, and bake for another 10-15 minutes.

plan ahead

Jamaican Spice Blend can be made ahead and stored in a tightly sealed container for up to 3-4 weeks.

simplify

No time to watch over your stew? Set it and forget it as a slow cooker recipe in your crockpot! Simply brown chicken as in directions at right, transfer to crock pot and add remaining ingredients (including raw sweet potatoes). Cook on low for 4 hours, adding more chicken broth as needed by the ¼ cupful if mixture looks dry.

coconut spiced chicken stew

Sweet and pungent, this stew is infused with a delightfully fresh flavor.

- 5 tablespoons peanut oil or vegetable oil, divided
- 3 sweet potatoes, peeled and cubed
- Kosher salt and freshly ground black pepper, to taste
- 2 pounds skinless, boneless chicken thighs, trimmed and cut into 1- to 2-inch pieces
- 1 bunch scallions, thinly sliced (dark green and white parts reserved separately)
- 1-inch piece fresh ginger, peeled and grated
- 2 cloves garlic, minced
- Jamaican Spice Blend *(recipe to the right)*
- 1½ cups low-sodium chicken broth, or more as needed
- 1 (28-ounce) can crushed tomatoes with liquid
- ⅓ cup dried tart cherries, finely chopped
- 1 green bell pepper, seeded and diced
- ⅓ cup unsweetened flaked coconut shavings, plus more for garnish

Brown sweet potatoes: Heat 3 tablespoons oil in a large heavy soup pot or Dutch Oven over medium-high heat. Add cubed sweet potatoes. Season with kosher salt and sauté until sweet potatoes begin to soften and turn golden, about 15 minutes. Transfer to a medium bowl.

Brown chicken: Return the pot to medium-high heat and add remaining 2 tablespoons oil. Add the chicken in a single layer on the bottom of the pot (you may need to do this in 2 batches). Season with kosher salt and sauté until chicken is lightly browned on all sides, about 6 minutes. Transfer chicken to a large bowl.

Stew: Reduce heat to medium and add white parts of scallions, ginger and garlic to the pot. Sauté until fragrant, about 1-2 minutes. Add Jamaican Spice Blend. Stir quickly to blend and then slowly pour in the chicken broth. Bring to a boil, scraping up any browned bits. Add crushed tomatoes; reduce heat to medium-low, cover, and simmer for 15 minutes. Stir in dried cherries, green pepper and coconut shavings. Return chicken and any accumulated juices to the pot. Cover and simmer 10 minutes. Add sautéed sweet potatoes to the pot. Cover and simmer until chicken is cooked through and sweet potatoes are tender, adding more chicken broth by ¼ cupfuls if mixture is dry, about 10 minutes longer. Season to taste with salt and pepper.

Serve: Sprinkle each serving with sliced green scallions and coconut shavings before serving.

Jamaican spice blend

- 1½ teaspoons ground coriander
- 1 teaspoon ground cumin
- ½ teaspoon freshly ground black pepper
- ½ teaspoon ground cloves
- ¾ teaspoon ground cinnamon
- ½ teaspoon turmeric
- ⅛-¼ teaspoon cayenne pepper

Combine all spices together in a small bowl.

chicken drummettes in root beer sauce

The secret to these finger-licking good chicken drummettes is the double marinade. The intense flavors will have people asking for seconds…and thirds!

- 1 tablespoon kosher salt
- 1 tablespoon paprika
- 1 tablespoon dark brown sugar
- 2 teaspoons ground black pepper
- ¼ teaspoon celery seed
- 20 chicken drummettes or 8 chicken quarters
- 1 cup water
- ¾ cup white vinegar
- ¼ cup soy sauce
- ½ teaspoon hickory smoke flavor
- Root beer sauce *(recipe below)*

Rub and Marinade: Combine salt, paprika, brown sugar, pepper and celery seed in small bowl. Reserve 4 teaspoons and set aside for marinade. Rub remaining spice mixture all over chicken drummettes or quarters. Refrigerate chicken for 1 hour. Combine water, vinegar, soy sauce, hickory smoke flavor and reserved 4 teaspoons spice mixture in medium mixing bowl. Stir to blend and pour over chicken. Marinate for at least 4 hours or overnight.

Broil: Preheat oven broiler to low. Remove chicken from marinade, discarding marinade. Place the prepared chicken pieces in a roasting pan and brush with root beer sauce. Broil for a total of about 40 minutes, turning and basting with remaining sauce every 10 minutes. If using chicken bottoms, you will need to add about 20 minutes to the broiling time.

prep time
30-40 minutes
plus marinating
time

cook time
40 minutes

serves
8

plan ahead

Spice rub and sauce can be made 2 weeks ahead; keep sauce refrigerated.

simplify

Combine rub ingredients and place on chicken. Refrigerate for 1-2 hours and proceed with Broil step. The flavor will not be as intense but will work in a pinch.

root beer sauce

- 1 cup root beer
- 2 tablespoons fresh lemon juice
- 2 tablespoons orange juice
- 1¼ cups plain barbecue sauce
- ½ teaspoon grated lemon peel
- ½ teaspoon ground ginger
- Freshly ground black pepper
- Kosher salt

Combine all sauce ingredients in a heavy medium saucepan. Bring to a boil over medium heat, stirring occasionally. Reduce heat to medium-low and simmer until reduced to 1½ cups, about 20 minutes. Season to taste with kosher salt and freshly ground black pepper. Cool slightly. If making ahead, transfer to a bowl, cover and refrigerate.

plan ahead

Chicken can be assembled up to a day ahead. Cover and refrigerate until cooking time.

pastrami chicken emballé

"Emballé" is French for "wrap"… When browned, pastrami takes on a decadently crisp texture, adding new depths of flavor and insulating moisture in this versatile chicken dish.

- ¾ cup mayonnaise
- ½ cup chives, chopped
- 1 teaspoon water
- 6 whole skinless, boneless chicken breasts, trimmed, pounded flat and cut in half
- Kosher salt
- Freshly ground black pepper
- 24 thin slices fresh-cut pastrami
- 2 tablespoons vegetable oil
- Caramelized Shallot Dressing *(optional, recipe to the right)*

Assembly: Combine mayonnaise, chives and water in a small bowl. Whisk to blend. Set aside. Cut a slit in each chicken breast beginning at the thicker end, approximately 2 inches long and 1 inch deep. Insert ½ tablespoon of mayonnaise mixture into the pocket and press closed. Season chicken with salt and freshly ground black pepper. Lay two pieces of pastrami next to each other, slightly overlapping on a work surface or sheet of waxed paper. Place a chicken breast across the center of the slices. Wrap the pastrami slices around the chicken, completely enclosing the chicken. Press to adhere to chicken. Place the chicken seam side down on a plate. Repeat with remaining chicken.

Brown & Bake: Preheat oven to 350°. Heat 1 tablespoon oil in a large skillet over medium-high heat. Add chicken breasts, seam side down, to each pan and cook until browned, about 4-5 minutes per side. You may need to do this in batches. Transfer to a foil-lined baking sheet and bake in preheated oven for 15-20 minutes (or longer, depending on the size of the chicken breast).

Serving Options: This recipe can be served as a salad entrée or appetizer. Slice chicken crosswise into thin strips and either arrange on a large platter or plate individually over a bed of shredded romaine or cole slaw mix. Drizzle with Caramelized Shallot Dressing.

caramelized shallot dressing

- 1½ tablespoons canola oil, divided
- 1 shallot, sliced
- 2 cloves garlic, minced
- ¼ cup may...
- 2 teaspoons ...
- Salt
- Freshly ground blac...

Heat 1 tablespoon of oil in a small frying pan over medium-high heat. Add shallot and garlic, and sauté until browned, about 6-8 minutes. Transfer to food processor and pureé together with remaining oil, mayonnaise and water. Season to taste with salt and freshly ground black pepper.

...lled honey basil chicken

...nd quick to prepare, this flavorful dish gets its kick from fresh basil and chili sauce.

...e (3-pound) chicken
..., thinly sliced
...basil leaves, chopped
...ounce) chili sauce
...ney
...garlic, minced
...n fresh basil leaves, minced

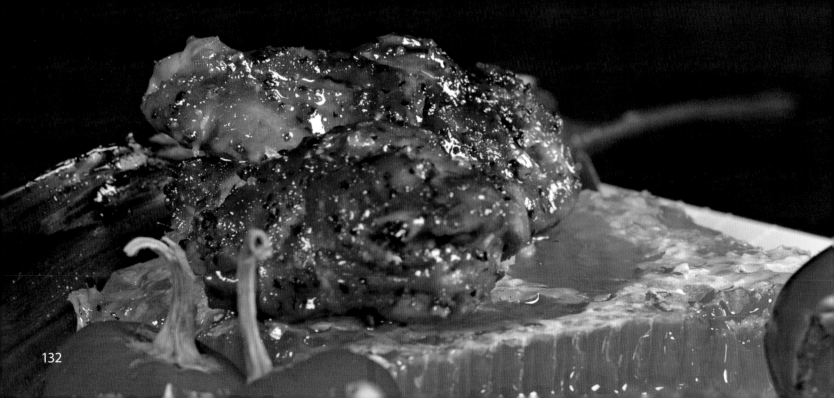

...advance and stored separately in the refrigerator.

simplify
Substitute 4 cubes frozen garlic for fresh; substitute 1 cube frozen basil for fresh.

Prep: Preheat broiler. On a flat work surface, arrange chicken breast side up. Carefully loosen the skin by running your fingers between the skin and flesh. Insert sliced onion and basil leaves just under the skin. Mix remaining ingredients in a small bowl and spread over chicken. Tuck the loose flap of skin over the cavity.

Broil: Place chicken in a roasting pan and place in the oven about 5 inches from the broiler. Broil, turning every 12 minutes for a total of 40–50 minutes or until juices run clear when pierced at the thigh. Remove from broiler and allow to rest for 10–15 minutes before serving time.

crunchy almond crusted chicken and mandarin orange salad

Panko bread crumbs are coarse Japanese bread crumbs, perfect for maintaining the crunchy texture of these well-seasoned chicken tenders within a dressed salad.

- 2 lbs. chicken breast tenders or cutlets, cut in long thin strips (appx. 4 inches long)
- 2 eggs
- 2 tablespoons teriyaki sauce
- 1 cup panko bread crumbs
- ¾ cup smoked almonds, toasted and finely chopped
- ¼ cup vegetable oil, plus more as needed
- 10 cups romaine hearts, thinly sliced
- 1 can mandarin orange segments, drained
- Sweet Teriyaki Dressing

sweet teriyaki dressing

- ½ cup teriyaki sauce
- ⅓ cup olive oil
- ¼ cup brown sugar
- ¼ cup cider vinegar
- 2 teaspoons orange peel, freshly grated

Whisk all ingredients together in a bowl until well blended.

Prepare the Chicken: Beat eggs with teriyaki sauce in a small bowl. Combine bread crumbs and almonds in a shallow dish. Dip chicken tenders into egg mixture and then into almond mixture. In a large skillet, heat oil over medium-high heat. Add prepared chicken tenders and cook until golden brown, about 4 minutes per side. Transfer to a paper towel-lined plate to drain. Repeat with remaining batches of tenders, adding more oil as needed for frying.

Assembly: Toss romaine with half of dressing in a large bowl and divide among individual serving plates. Arrange chicken and mandarin orange segments on romaine and drizzle each plate with remaining dressing.

chicken breast with avocado pomegranate relish

A must when pomegranates are in season — bold and fresh flavors make this dish stand out. When at the market, look for a firm pomegranate with smooth, unwrinkled skin.

- ½ cup lemon juice
- 5 tablespoons extra-virgin olive oil, divided
- 5 tablespoons pomegranate syrup or molasses
- 1 teaspoon kosher salt

- ½ teaspoon freshly ground black pepper
- 8 skinless boneless chicken breasts, trimmed and pounded thin
- Avocado Pomegranate Relish *(recipe below)*

garnish
- Chopped cilantro

prep time
15 minutes
plus 1 hour
marinating time

cook time
10 minutes

serves
8

plan ahead
Relish can be made 4 hours ahead-store refrigerated in tightly sealed container with avocado pits to retain green color.

simplify
Use ready-made chicken cutlets and serve with the fresh relish.

Marinate: In a zip top plastic bag, combine lemon juice, 3 tablespoons olive oil, pomegranate syrup, salt and pepper. Add chicken pieces and shake until well coated. Marinate up to 1 hour.

Sear Chicken: Heat 1 tablespoon olive oil in a large skillet over medium heat. Cook chicken breasts until lightly browned, about 3-4 minutes per side for thin breasts. Repeat with remaining breasts, adding more olive oil to pan as needed. To serve, spoon avocado pomegranate relish over warm chicken. Garnish plate with chopped cilantro.

Serving Options: For a fun lunch entreé, slice chicken breasts into strips and place into a taco or soft tortilla. Top with fresh relish.

avocado pomegranate relish
This flavorful relish could stand alone, but is an especially refreshing contrast when served with the warm chicken breasts.

- 1 large lemon
- 2 cloves garlic, minced
- Seeds from 1 pomegranate
- 6 scallions, white and light green parts only, thinly sliced
- 2 avocados (not overly ripe), peeled, pitted and diced

- ¼ cup extra-virgin olive oil
- ¼ cup parsley, chopped
- 5 tablespoons cilantro, chopped plus more for garnish
- 2 teaspoons pomegranate syrup
- 1 teaspoon kosher salt
- Freshly ground black pepper, to taste

Working over a small bowl, zest and juice the lemon. Add remaining ingredients. Stir to blend and season to taste.

prep time
10 minutes plus extra time for cleaning and marinating chicken wings

cook time
30-35 minutes

serves
6

plan ahead

Wings can be made up to 2 days in advance.

ginger glazed sesame chicken wings

Flavorful and bold, tangy and sweet, these wings are a real crowd pleaser, appealing to guests both young and old.

- 16 chicken wings
- 1 cup soy sauce
- ¼ cup honey
- ⅓ cup cider vinegar
- 1¼ tablespoons fresh ginger, peeled and chopped
- ¼ cup sesame oil
- 1 clove garlic, minced
- ¼ cup sesame seeds

Clean: Rinse chicken and pat dry. Clean and trim wings thoroughly, removing pinfeathers. Place wings in a shallow glass baking dish.

Marinate: Combine soy sauce, honey, vinegar, ginger, sesame oil and garlic in a medium bowl. Whisk until well blended, and pour over chicken. Marinate overnight, or for at least 4 hours.

Bake: Preheat oven to 425°. Turn chicken wings to coat with marinade and sprinkle with sesame seeds. Bake uncovered for 20 minutes. Baste with pan juices and bake for an additional 10-15 minutes or until wings are browned and cooked through. Remove from oven and serve.

Serving Option: To serve as an hors d'oeuvre, cut the wings in half at the joint for bite-size pieces. Better yet, save yourself the work, and request that your butcher split the wings — order ahead!

turkey and pastrami rollatini

An appealing alternative to chicken cutlets, turkey complements the flavor of the past... *beautifully in this elegant breaded entrée.*

- 2 pounds turkey cutlets, pounded thin
- Kosher salt and freshly ground black pepper, to taste
- 8 slices pastrami, thinly sliced
- 10 scallions, green part only
- ½ cup light mayonnaise
- 2 teaspoons mustard
- ⅔ cup seasoned bread crumbs
- 5 tomatoes, seeded and diced *(optional)*

prep time
30 minutes

cook time
approximately
30 minutes

serves
6-8

refrigera...
baking time.

Prep: Preheat oven to 350°. Grease a large baking dish. Set aside.

Assemble: Lay cutlets flat on a clean working surface or cutting board. Cut cutlets in two if very large or thick and season with salt and freshly ground black pepper. Place a piece of pastrami on top of each cutlet. Lay the scallion over the center of the pastrami and starting at narrowest end, roll up cutlets. The scallion should protrude slightly from either end.

Place mayonnaise and mustard in a small bowl, whisking to blend. Place bread crumbs in a separate shallow dish. Lightly dip rolled cutlets in the mayonnaise mixture, then dredge in crumbs. Place breaded rolled cutlets in the prepared baking dish, seam side down. Place a toothpick in the center of each roll for a secure seal.

Bake: Bake uncovered for about 25 minutes, until lightly browned and turkey is cooked through. Remove from oven. Prior to serving, remove toothpicks.

Serving Option: To serve, place rollatini on a bed of diced tomatoes.

triple citrus glazed cornish hens

Trapped in the browned bits littering your pan following roasting or browning of meats are the most deliciously concentrated flavors. There they lie, just waiting for the chance to make your sauce great…but how? Deglazing is the process of heating a liquid and stirring to loosen these browned bits, essentially melting and dissolving them to form a new gravy or sauce. Wine or stock are typically used, but here citrus juices do the trick.

- 2 oranges
- 1 lemon
- 1 lime
- 2 tablespoons canola oil, divided
- 4 cloves garlic, minced
- 2 shallots, thinly sliced
- 1½ teaspoons sugar
- 4 Cornish hens, about 1¼ pounds each
- Kosher salt and freshly ground black pepper, to taste
- 2 limes, peeled and cut into small sections (pith removed)

Prep: Preheat oven to 500°.

Citrus Glaze: Zest oranges, lemon and lime and reserve in a small bowl. Heat 1 tablespoon of oil in a heavy skillet over medium heat. Add garlic and shallots, sautéing about 2-3 minutes or until shallots begin to brown. Add the juice of the zested citrus fruits and sugar; bring to a boil. Let cool and set aside.

Brown: Rinse hens and pat dry. Season hens with salt and pepper. In a separate large skillet, heat remaining tablespoon of oil over high heat. Brown hens in the skillet, about 6 minutes per side. Transfer hens to a large low-rimmed pan (such as a jelly roll pan), and place hens breast-side up. Reserve the skillet for later use.

Roast: Pour half of citrus glaze over hens. Scatter lime pieces over hens and roast until hens are cooked through, about 25 minutes. Remove from oven and allow to rest for 10 minutes. Meanwhile, return reserved skillet to the stovetop over medium-high heat. Add remaining half of citrus glaze, stirring and scraping up browned bits until fully dissolved into the sauce, about 1-2 minutes. Transfer hens to a serving platter and pour glaze over. To serve, sprinkle reserved tri-colored zests over hens.

...w ahead

...itrus Glaze can be prepared a day ahead; store in the refrigerator. Deglaze just before serving.

simplify

Substitute ½ cup prepared lemonade for lime juice, lemon juice and sugar.

golden duck with orange paprika glaze

prep time
5 minutes plus
basting time

cook time
1 hour,
30 minutes

serves
4

A centerpiece entrée. This is a no-fail duck recipe that anyone can make!

- 1 whole duck, cleaned with pinfeathers removed
- 6 cloves garlic, minced
- ¼ cup paprika
- ½ cup orange juice
- ¼ cup duck sauce

Prep: Preheat oven to 400°. Place the duck, breast side up, in a large baking dish. In a small bowl, mix together the garlic and paprika. Add orange juice slowly until a liquid paste forms. With a pastry brush the paste over both sides of the duck.

Bake: Cover and bake duck for 1 hour. Reduce oven temperature to 350°. Uncover duck and continue to bake for an additional 30 minutes, turning midway. Brush duck sauce on duck, and bake for another 10 minutes. Duck should be golden brown in color with a nicely glazed skin. Remove from oven and allow duck to rest for 10 minutes before serving.

plan ahead
Ducks are infamous for their numerous pinfeathers and can be time consuming to clean. Use tweezers for an easier prep.

cook's note
If making in advance, brush duck sauce on duck just prior to reheating. Reheat at 350° uncovered.

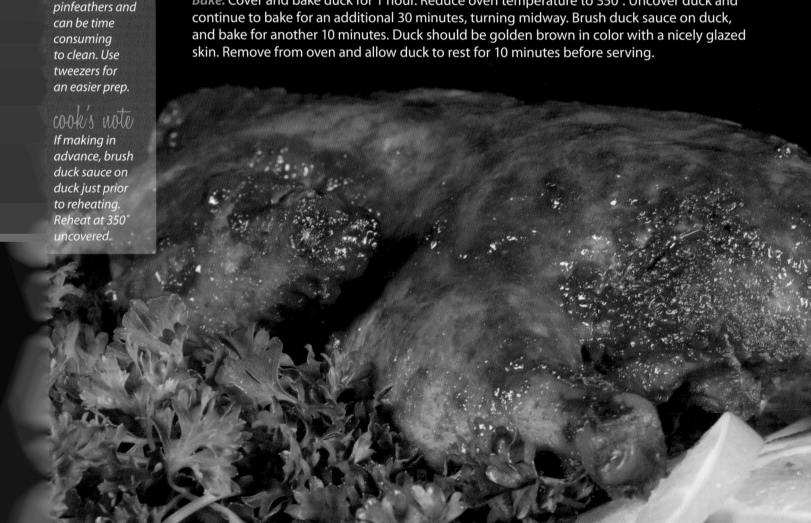

sweet and sticky turkey drumsticks

Simple to prepare, this sweet and tangy dish is a great alternative to chicken any night of the

- 2 tablespoons olive oil
- 1 medium onion, **diced**
- 1 (16-ounce) can whole berry cranberry sauce
- ⅓ cup apricot preserves
- ⅓ cup ketchup
- 1 tablespoon fresh lemon juice (**from about ½ lemon**)
- 1 (8-ounce) can tomato sauce
- 8 turkey drumsticks

Prep: Preheat oven to 350°.

Sauce: In a medium saucepan, heat oil over medium-high heat. Add onion and sauté until onion begins to brown, around 15 minutes. Add cranberry sauce, apricot preserves, ketchup, lemon juice and tomato sauce. Stir over medium heat until the ingredients are well blended. Remove from heat.

Bake: Place turkey drumsticks in a 9"x 13" glass baking dish. Pour cranberry-apricot sauce over the turkey and bake covered for 45 minutes. Uncover and continue to bake for an additional 25 minutes, turning the drumsticks once halfway through.

can be pre... up to 2 days in advance.

143

asian stir-fry with crisp vegetables

This is a basic stir-fry recipe that is easily adaptable, utilizing whatever vegetables you happen to have on hand or enjoy. For no-fail results, always add vegetables in order of longest to shortest cooking time, adding hard vegetables like carrots or peppers first, and softer vegetables like mushrooms or snow peas toward the end of cooking time.

prep time
15 minutes

cook time
15-20 minutes

serves
4

- 1 (16-ounce) can low-sodium chicken broth
- 2 tablespoons cornstarch
- 2 tablespoons soy sauce
- ½ teaspoon ground ginger
- 2 tablespoons canola oil
- 2 cloves garlic, minced
- 2 pounds boneless, skinless chicken breasts, cut into thin strips
- 6 cups assorted fresh vegetables, such as snow peas, broccoli florets and mushrooms

Sauce: In a small bowl, stir broth, cornstarch, soy sauce and ginger together until smooth and set aside.

Stir-fry: In a large frying pan or wok, heat oil over medium-high heat. Add garlic, sautéing until golden and popping, about 2-3 minutes. Add chicken and stir rapidly until browned and cooked halfway through, about 6 minutes. Add vegetables and continue to stir-fry for 5-10 minutes, or until vegetables are tender crisp.

Finish: Stir sauce and add to the skillet. Stirring constantly, bring to a boil and simmer for 1 minute or until sauce thickens.

plan ahead

Prepare your vegetables a day ahead and refrigerate until cooking time.

simplify

2 bags frozen assorted vegetables, defrosted, may be used instead of fresh vegetables.

plan ahead

Cranberry-chili sauce can be prepared up to 4 days ahead and stored in a tightly covered container in the refrigerator.

savory cranberry turkey wraps

Put an end to those lunchbox blues with these wraps! Nutritious and simple to prepare, it's time to breathe some new inspiration into yesterday's sandwich.

- 1 cup chili sauce
- ½ cup fresh or frozen cranberries (defrosted)
- 8 plain or flavored wraps
- 1 container alfalfa sprouts
- 2 ripe avocados, peeled, pitted and diced
- 6 scallions, sliced lengthwise into long, thin strips
- 16 ounces sliced smoked turkey breast

Prepare sauce: Bring the chili sauce and cranberries to a simmer in a small saucepan over medium heat, stirring to blend (about 5 minutes). Remove from heat and cool.

Assembly: Spread 2 tablespoons of cranberry-chili sauce onto each wrap. Top each with a handful of alfalfa sprouts, avocado and scallions, leaving a 1-inch border on one end of the wrap. Layer approximately 4 slices of the turkey breast over the vegetable filling. Roll up tightly toward the side with border. Wrap each in plastic wrap and refrigerate at least 15 minutes. Cut diagonally into halves and serve.

roasted chicken skewers
with almonds and dried fruit

Studded with aromatic dried fruits, these sweet skewers are infused with flavor in each bite. Serve with Coconut Jasmine rice (page 214) as a fine accompaniment.

- 20 long bamboo skewers
- 12 ounces pitted prunes (about 2½ cups)
- 10 ounces pitted dates (about 2 cups), **halved**
- 8 ounces dried apricots (about 1½ cups)
- 3 tablespoons sugar
- 1 teaspoon ground cinnamon
- 2½ pounds skinless, **boneless chicken thighs, trimmed and cut evenly into 1½-inch chunks**
- 3 tablespoons olive oil
- 1 teaspoon turmeric
- ½ teaspoon kosher salt
- ½ teaspoon ground black pepper
- ½ cup blanched slivered almonds, **toasted and finely chopped**

Set up: Arrange oven rack on the second-to-highest shelf in the oven. Preheat broiler to low. Prepare a large rimmed pan lined with foil. Set aside. Soak bamboo skewers in a pan of water for about 15-20 minutes.

Prepare chicken: Combine the first five ingredients in a medium bowl, and toss until combined. In a separate bowl, toss chicken with olive oil, turmeric, salt and pepper. Thread chicken pieces and fruit onto the bamboo skewers, placing a piece of fruit between each chicken piece. Arrange skewers on the prepared pan.

Broil: Broil chicken skewers for 8-10 minutes, turning after 4 minutes. Remove from heat. Sprinkle with almonds and serve.

plan ahead

Skewers can be prepared a day ahead. Cover with plastic wrap and refrigerate.

simplify

If time does not allow for soaking the skewers, cover ends of skewers with foil after placing food on the skewers to prevent burning.

...der basil chicken burgers

...for a healthy alternative to beef burgers? Even the most die-hard beef fans
...this bold burger redux for a quick weeknight supper!

prep time
25 minutes
...ook time
...0 minutes

- ...ground chicken
- *(recipe below)*
- ...d black pepper
- ...buns
- ...ve oil (for brushing)
- 3-inch flat cracker rounds (optional)
- 1 large red heirloom tomato, cut into 4 (1/3-inch-thick) slices
- 16 large basil leaves

...tainer for
up to 1 week.

Prep: Preheat oven to 400°. Prepare Basil Relish.

Prep: Mix chicken and ¾ cup Basil Relish in a large bowl. Season with salt and pepper. Using wet hands, gently shape chicken mixture into eight ½-inch-thick patties. For best results, do not over-compact. Place patties on foil-lined baking sheet.

Roast: Brush hamburger buns with oil and toast in oven for 4 minutes. Place burgers in oven and roast uncovered until firm to the touch and cooked through, about 6 minutes per side, depending on thickness.

Assembly: Spread a thick layer of Basil Relish over each bun bottom. Then layer each with cracker, tomato slice, 2 basil leaves, burger, a dollop of relish and bun top.

Serving Option: For fun party fare or hors d'oeuvres, shape ground chicken mixture into sliders (mini-sized patties). Serve on slider buns, *(recipe on page 25)* and top as directed above.

basil relish

- 1½ cups mayonnaise
- 2 cups chopped fresh basil leaves
- ⅓ cup chopped dill pickles plus
  3 tablespoons pickle juice reserved from can
- 4 scallions, thinly sliced
- Kosher salt and freshly ground black pepper, to taste

Mix mayonnaise, chopped basil, chopped pickles, pickle juice, and scallions in small bowl. Season to taste with salt and pepper.

meat

mini veal meatball skewers
with sesame-lime sauce

Skewers make for easy serving and fun eating – jazz up your table with these Asian-inspired skewers as a main, or serve plated with sauce as an appetizer.

prep time
15 minutes

cook time
20 minutes

serves
6

plan ahead

Meatball mixture can be prepared a day ahead.

- ½ cup soy milk
- ½ cup fine dry bread crumbs
- 1½ pounds ground veal
- 1 large egg, lightly beaten
- 1 cup (about 10 ounces) canned sliced water chestnuts, rinsed, drained, and finely chopped
- 1¼ teaspoons salt
- ¾ cup chopped fresh cilantro

- 2 tablespoons soy sauce
- 4 teaspoons sesame oil

special equipment
- Mini bamboo skewers or long skewers

garnish
- 6 limes cut into eighths, ¼ cup cilantro sprigs
- Sesame-Lime sauce *(recipe below)*

Prep: Preheat oven to 500°. Line a baking sheet with foil and spray with cooking spray.

Meatballs: In a large mixing bowl, combine all ingredients and mix until combined well. Using slightly wet hands , shape approximately 1½ tablespoons of the meat mixture into a ball and place on skewer, separating each meatball with a piece of lime. Allow 3 meatballs per mini skewer; six per large skewer. Transfer to a greased baking sheet. Repeat with remaining mixture, arranging skewers about ½-inch apart on baking sheet.

Bake: Bake until cooked through, about 15 minutes. Meanwhile, prepare Sesame-Lime Sauce (recipe below).

Serve: Transfer meatball skewers to a serving dish. Drizzle sauce over skewers and garnish with cilantro sprigs.

sesame lime sauce

- ¼ cup fresh lime juice
- ¼ cup water
- 4 teaspoons sugar
- ½ cup soy sauce
- 4 teaspoons sesame oil

Stir together all ingredients in a small mixing bowl until sugar is dissolved.

prep time
10 minutes

cook time
6-7 minutes

serves
2 as a main dish
4 as an appetizer

baby lamb chops
in fresh herb chimichurri

CONTRIBUTED BY AVI PIFKO, GRILLING EXPERT AND AFICIONADO

Chimichurri is an Argentinian sauce or marinade used for grilled meat. It is usually made with garlic, oil and fresh herbs and flavorings. Ours does double duty and is a zesty complement to baby lamb chops.

- ½ cup extra-virgin olive oil
- 2 cloves garlic, minced
- 2 tablespoons freshly squeezed lemon juice (from 1 lemon)
- ½ teaspoon lemon zest, finely grated
- 1 teaspoon honey
- ¼ cup minced fresh mint
- ¼ cup minced fresh parsley
- 1 teaspoon minced fresh rosemary
- 1 teaspoon minced fresh oregano
- Kosher salt and freshly ground black pepper, to taste
- 6 single cut baby lamb chops, frenched

Prep: Combine first 9 ingredients in a small bowl. Mix until a paste-like consistency is reached. Season with salt and pepper.

Marinate: Pour most of the chimichurri over lamb chops, reserving a small amount for later use. Coat both sides of lamb chops with chimichurri, and marinate at room temperature for 30 minutes, or cover and refrigerate up to 2 hours.

Grill: Preheat grill to medium-high. Place lamb chops on grill for about 2-3 minutes per side, turning only once during grilling for medium-rare to medium doneness. Remove from grill and serve with reserved chimichurri.

plan ahead

Chimichurri can be made up to 3 days ahead. Store in a tightly sealed container in the refrigerator.

simplify

Chimichurri can also be prepared in the food processor.

cook's note

To "French" means to cut the meat away from the end of a rib or chop so that part of the bone is exposed. Your butcher will be happy to do this upon request.

the butcher's french roast

ADAPTED FROM A RECIPE BY LAIBI KRAITENBERG, NETZACH ISRAEL MEATS, BROOKLYN, NY

The recipe for this simple roast comes from the butcher himself!
This is a great "go-to" recipe for serving a crowd – no fail, and no fuss!

- 2 onions, sliced into rings
- 2 tomatoes, sliced into rings
- 1 (5-pound) French roast or square-cut roast
- 1½ cups duck sauce
- 1½ cups dry red wine
- 1 tablespoon onion powder
- 2 teaspoons garlic powder
- 2 teaspoons paprika

Prep: Place half of the onions and half of the tomatoes in a large roasting pan. Place roast on top, covering with the remaining tomatoes and onions. Pour duck sauce and wine over roast and season with onion powder, garlic powder and paprika. Cover, refrigerate and marinate for at least 2 hours or overnight.

Bake: Preheat oven to 375°. Bring roast to room temperature and place in oven. Bake covered for about 3 hours, 15 minutes or until tender when pierced with a fork. Remove from oven and cool. Transfer to a cutting board, and using a sharp carving knife, slice thinly across the grain. Place slices on a serving platter and dress with sauce.

prep time
10 minutes

cook time
3 hours,
15 minutes

serves
8

cook's note

This roast freezes beautifully. Cover well. Defrost in the refrigerator for 1½ days.

prep time
20 minutes plus
marinating time

cook time
2 hours,
30 minutes

serves
6-8

spiced brisket with dried fruits

CONTRIBUTED BY NAOMI ROSS, COOKING INSTRUCTOR AND FOOD WRITER

This braised meat is packed with flavor after marinating in an aromatic spice rub overnight. This recipe can be used interchangeably with French roast. Amounts double easily for a larger cut of meat.

- 2 teaspoons coarse kosher salt
- 1 teaspoon ground coriander
- ¾ teaspoon ground cumin
- ½ teaspoon freshly ground black pepper
- 1 teaspoon ground cinnamon
- ¼ teaspoon ground nutmeg
- ½ teaspoon ground allspice
- 1 (3-pound) first-cut brisket
- 2-3 tablespoons canola or vegetable oil
- 2 medium onions, sliced (about 3 cups)
- 4 cloves garlic, chopped
- 1 cup dry red wine

- 2 small or 1 large parsnip, peeled and cut into 1-inch pieces
- 2 small or 1 large carrot, peeled and cut into 1-inch pieces
- ½ cup whole pitted prunes
- ½ cup dried apricots
- 2 tablespoons water
- 1½ tablespoons honey
- 1 tablespoon tomato paste

garnish
- Fresh parsley, chopped

Spice rub: Combine salt, coriander, cumin, pepper, cinnamon, nutmeg and allspice in a small bowl. Arrange brisket in a large roasting pan; rub spice mixture evenly over both sides. Cover and refrigerate overnight.

Brown: Preheat oven to 325°. Heat 2 tablespoons of oil in a very large skillet over high heat. Carefully place brisket in the skillet and brown for 1-2 minutes per side, turning once. Remove brisket from the skillet and transfer to a plate; set aside.

Sauté: Lower heat to medium and add another tablespoon of oil to the skillet if it looks dry. Add onions and garlic to the pan and sauté, stirring often and scraping up the browned bits at the bottom of the skillet. Sauté until translucent, about 5-6 minutes. Pour wine into the skillet and deglaze, scraping up the browned bits at the bottom of the skillet. Bring to a boil and simmer for 1-2 minutes. Place mixture in the bottom of a roasting pan and place brisket on top, fat side up. Surround brisket with parsnips, carrots, prunes and apricots.

Braise: In a small bowl, mix together water, honey and tomato paste. Stir to blend and then pour over the top of brisket, spreading to cover. Cover pan tightly with foil and bake until tender, about 2 hours, 30 minutes. Allow meat to rest and cool, about 30 minutes.

Serve: Transfer brisket to a cutting board and, using a very sharp carving knife, thinly slice brisket across the grain on a slight diagonal. Place slices back into the roasting pan. Place vegetables around meat and cover with pan juices. Cover and reheat before serving time. Transfer to a serving platter, garnish with chopped parsley and serve.

kalbi kui ribs

prep time
5 minutes

cook time
15-20 minutes

serves
8

Kalbi kui is Korean for grilled ribs - seriously delicious marinated ribs. Get your napkins ready! The uniqueness of this cut does away with the usual layer of fat and chewy meat that most ribs have, yielding a flatter, more tender rib.

- 1 cup soy sauce
- ½ cup mirin wine or sweet sherry
- ½ cup packed dark brown sugar
- ¼ cup unseasoned rice vinegar
- ¼ cup toasted or spicy sesame oil

- 16 cloves garlic, minced
- 3 scallions, thinly sliced
- 3 pounds beef chuck, also known as cross-cut short ribs, cut ⅓- to ½-inch thick across the bones

Prep: In a medium bowl, combine first 7 ingredients and whisk to blend. Pour into a large zip top bag, add ribs and marinate, turning to coat. Refrigerate overnight, turning occasionally.

Broil: Preheat oven broiler. Remove ribs, reserving marinade. Place ribs in a broiler pan and broil until brown. Turn over and brush with marinade once during broiling (broil 7 minutes per side for medium-rare, 9 minutes per side for medium-well, 11 minutes per side for well-done).

Sauce: Place marinade in a small sauce pan and boil over medium heat for 4 minutes. Serve alongside or drizzled over ribs.

rib eye in maple soy sauce marinade

CONTRIBUTED BY AVI PIFKO, GRILLING EXPERT AND AFICIONADO

Maple and soy are the perfect combination of salty and sweet for these mouth-watering steaks.

- ½ cup soy sauce
- ¼ cup pure maple syrup
- 1 teaspoon dark sesame oil
- 4 cloves garlic, **minced**
- 1 tablespoon fresh ginger, peeled and grated

- 1 teaspoon dry mustard
- ¼ teaspoon hot pepper sauce
- ¼ cup beer
- 2 rib eye beef steaks, approximately 1½-inch thick

prep time
5-10 minutes plus marinating time

cook time
10-15 minutes

serves
2

Prep: Combine first 8 ingredients in a large bowl or container, mixing well to combine.

Marinate: Add steaks to the marinade, turning to coat. Cover and marinate for at least 1 hour and up to 8 hours in the refrigerator.

Grill: Preheat grill to high. Grill steaks for 5 minutes on each side, turning once. Reduce heat to medium-low and continue to grill for 4-5 additional minutes for medium-rare. Remove steaks from grill and allow to rest for 5-10 minutes before serving.

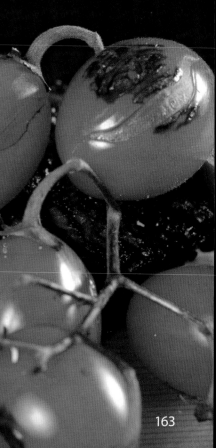

prep time
10 minutes plus
marinating time

cook time
20-25 minutes

serves
6 as a starter
8 as a salad

plan ahead

Dressing can be prepared a day ahead and stored in tightly covered container in the refrigerator.

grilled teriyaki steak salad

A grill pan is a great alternative to outdoor grilling, especially in the winter months. Perfect grill marks and flavor can be achieved in the comfort of your own kitchen.

- 1½ pounds oyster steak or fillet steak, sliced into ½-inch-thick strips
- Freshly ground black pepper, to taste
- ½ cup teriyaki sauce, divided
- ⅓ cup peanut oil
- ¼ cup freshly lime juice (from about 2-3 limes)
- 2 tablespoons dark brown sugar
- Kosher salt, to taste
- 2 heads romaine hearts, shredded
- ½ head purple cabbage, shredded
- 1 small red onion, sliced into thin rings (about ½ cup)

garnish
- Toasted slivered almonds

Marinate: Place steak in a shallow container and season with pepper. Add ¼ cup teriyaki sauce and turn steak to coat. Set aside to marinate for 15-20 minutes.

Grill: Preheat a grill pan over medium-high heat. Add the steak, reserving the marinade, and cook for about 15-20 minutes, stirring occasionally. The steak should be nicely browned and tender. In the last few minutes of cooking time, drizzle 3-4 tablespoons of the reserved marinade into the pan. Continue to cook, turning frequently, until steak sauce is reduced and steak is nicely glazed. Remove from heat.

Salad: Combine oil, lime juice, brown sugar and remaining ¼ cup teriyaki sauce in a small bowl, whisking to blend until smooth. Season with salt and pepper. Pour half of the dressing in a large bowl and combine with romaine, cabbage and onion.

Assembly: If serving individually plated, divide the salad amongst the plates, mounding the mixture in the center of each plate. Arrange the steak slices on top of the cabbage mixture. Drizzle the remaining dressing and any pan juices over the salad. Garnish with toasted slivered almonds and serve.

Serving Option: Mound the salad into a high pyramid. Lay the strips of meat vertically from the top of the pyramid, around the salad, as a beautiful starter course.

short ribs
in red wine and mushroom sauce

Your crock pot is not just for cholent anymore! Prepare this full flavored dish in the morning and forget about it until you come home to a gourmet meal in the evening…

prep time
5 minutes

cook time
8 hours

serves
8

- 6 pounds (3-inch-long) beef short ribs
- Kosher salt and freshly ground black pepper, to taste
- 3½-4 cups Merlot or other good quality dry red wine
- 2 (14.5-ounce) cans diced tomatoes, undrained
- 1 (6-ounce) package sliced button mushrooms
- 1 cup onion, finely chopped (about 1 small onion)
- 10 cloves garlic, peeled
- 12 fresh Italian parsley sprigs
- 2 bay leaves

Prep: Season ribs with salt and pepper. Place in an even layer a crock pot. Add remaining ingredients, cover and cook on low heat until meat is tender, about 8 hours.

Serve: Using slotted spoon, transfer ribs to a serving bowl. Discard parsley and bay leaves. Skim excess fat off the top of the sauce and season with salt and pepper. Pour sauce over ribs.

Serving Options: Serve over a bed of mashed potatoes or couscous.

simplify

Place parsley and bay leaves in a garnet bag or wrap securely in cheesecloth before cooking for easy removal.

cook's note

This dish is very fatty. If making ahead, refrigerate and remove top layer of congealed fat before serving.

prep time
25 minutes

cook time
3 hours,
30 minutes

serves
6

veal breast with savory vegetable-matzah stuffing

A wonderful holiday dish, this is a crowd pleaser any time of the year and is kosher for Passover as well.

savory vegetable-matzah stuffing

- ¼ cup olive oil
- 2 celery stalks, diced
- 2 carrots, chopped
- 2 medium onions, diced
- 3 matzahs, broken into small pieces
- 2 tablespoons parsley, chopped
- 1 large egg, lightly beaten
- ¾ teaspoon kosher salt
- ¼ teaspoon freshly ground black pepper

veal breast

- 1 small onion, quartered
- 2 cloves garlic, peeled
- 1 tablespoon olive oil
- 2 teaspoons paprika
- 1½ teaspoons salt
- 1 teaspoon freshly ground black pepper
- 1 (4-pound) boneless veal breast
- 2 sprigs fresh thyme
- 1½ cups dry white wine

Stuffing: Heat oil in a large Dutch Oven or ovenproof stockpot over medium heat. Add celery, carrots and onions; sauté, stirring occasionally, until vegetables are tender, about 8-10 minutes. Meanwhile, place matzah in a colander and run under hot water until softened. Drain and set aside. Remove pot from heat and transfer half of the vegetables to a bowl (reserving the remainder in the pot for later use). Cool for 5 minutes and add matzah, parsley, egg, salt and pepper. Set aside.

Prep: Preheat oven to 350°. Pureé onion, garlic, oil, paprika, salt and pepper in a food processor (fitted with "S" blade).

Fill: Place veal breast on a cutting board. Trim excess fat from veal. Starting from the short end of the breast, cut a large pocket in the veal, leaving a 1-inch border on 3 sides and being careful not to cut through to the other side. Spread 2 tablespoons of the pureé inside the pocket. Then fill the pocket loosely with stuffing, leaving a 1-inch border on cut side. Sew the pocket closed with kitchen string and a heavy needle (alternatively, close securely with toothpicks).

Pat veal dry and rub both sides with remaining pureé. Put thyme sprigs over vegetables remaining in the pot, top with veal. Add wine and bring to a boil over medium heat. If very dry, add water by ¼ cupfuls.

Braise: Cover the pot and transfer to the center of the oven, simmering until meat is very tender, about 3-3½ hours. Remove from oven and let stand for 30 minutes. Transfer veal to a cutting board, discarding thyme sprigs and string. Using a sharp carving knife, slice veal across the grain and serve with cooking liquid.

slow roasted bbq minute roast

CONTRIBUTED BY NAOMI ROSS, COOKING INSTRUCTOR AND FOOD WRITER

A flavorful homemade barbecue sauce glazes this tender roast, adding a boost of flavor. As it reduces during the long cooking time, it will become deliciously concentrated.

prep time
25 minutes

cook time
6 hours

serves
8

- 2 tablespoons vegetable oil, divided
- 1 large onion, chopped (about 1½ cups)
- ¾ cup red wine vinegar
- 1½ cups ketchup
- ⅓ cup molasses
- ⅓ cup water
- ½ cup bourbon
- 1 teaspoon salt
- Scant ½ teaspoon black pepper
- ¾ teaspoon dried thyme
- 1 (3½-4 pound) minute roast
- Freshly ground black pepper, to taste

Prepare sauce: Heat 1 tablespoon oil in a large, heavy saucepan over medium-high heat. Add onion and sauté until translucent, about 6 minutes. Add vinegar, ketchup, molasses, water, bourbon, salt, pepper and thyme. Stir to blend, and bring to a boil. Reduce heat to low and simmer for about 10 minutes to blend flavors.

Sear: Preheat oven to 225°. Place 1-2 teaspoons oil in a large skillet on high heat. Place minute roast in the skillet and brown, turning once, about 1-2 minutes per side. Transfer roast to a rack and place in a large roasting pan. Rub a small amount of oil (about 1-2 teaspoons) all over roast and season with pepper.

Slow-Roasting Magic: Pour sauce over roast and bake uncovered for 6 hours (or longer if you like it well-done), basting occasionally. Test for doneness with a meat thermometer – internal temperature will be your deciding factor (145° = rare, 160° = medium, 170° = well-done). The larger the roast, the longer the cooking time. Remove from oven and tent foil over roast, allowing roast to rest for 15-20 minutes. Slice roast and serve with remaining sauce from the roasting pan.

plan ahead

Sauce can be prepared a day ahead. Cover and refrigerate.

cook's note

This can be easily prepared overnight if timed properly – put it in to slow-roast before bedtime and take it out when you wake up (omit basting).

prep time
10 minutes

cook time
2 hours,
30 minutes

serves
8

brisket with caramelized mustard seeds

The full-bodied taste of mustard comes through when paired with brown sugar, accenting the natural sweetness of the brisket.

- ¼ cup water
- 1 cup brown sugar, divided
- ¼ cup whole mustard seeds
- ¾ cup (6 ounces) cream soda

- 1 teaspoon Dijon mustard
- ½ cup ketchup
- ¼ cup balsamic vinegar
- 1 (5-pound) first-cut brisket

Prep: Preheat oven to 400°.

Sauce: Bring water and ½ cup brown sugar to a boil in a small saucepan over medium heat, stirring constantly. Allow mixture to boil for 45 seconds without stirring. Remove from heat and add whole mustard seeds. Stir until combined. Set aside.

Bake: Combine soda, mustard, ½ cup brown sugar, ketchup and vinegar in a small bowl, whisking to blend. Place brisket in a large roasting pan, fat side up. Pour soda mixture over brisket. Slightly stir mustard seed mixture and spread over the top of brisket to coat. Cover tightly with foil and bake for 2 hours, 30 minutes, or until tender when pierced with a fork. Allow meat to rest and cool, about 30 minutes.

Serve: When cool, transfer brisket to a cutting board and thinly slice against the grain with a sharp carving knife. Platter and drizzle pan juices over the meat slices.

slow cooked corned beef in wine

*A long, low braise in wine yields deep flavor with tender, delicate results.
This is simplicity at its best.*

prep time
5 minutes
cook time
6 hours,
10 minutes
serves
8

- 2 tablespoons olive oil
- 1 (5-pound) first-cut corned beef
- ½-¾ bottle good quality dry red wine

Brown: Heat oil in a large skillet over medium-high heat. Add corned beef and brown on both sides, about 5-7 minutes. Transfer corned beef and pan drippings to a roasting pan.

Bake: Preheat oven to 300°. Pour wine over corned beef. Cover tightly with foil and bake for 6 hours. Remove from oven, cool and slice.

Serving Option: For a delicious accompanying sauce, simply pour the cooking liquid into a saucepan and bring to a boil over medium-low heat. Simmer for about 15-20 minutes or until mixture is reduced by half and is a thick syrupy consistency. Season to taste with salt and freshly ground black pepper.

sweet sausage meat loaf

Homey and satisfying, here's an updated version of a timeless classic…
it's not your mother's meatloaf anymore!

prep time
15 minutes

cook time
1 hour,
15 minutes

serves
8

- 2 pounds lean ground beef (15% fat)
- 2 small zucchini, peeled and finely shredded (about 2 cups)
- 1 pound sweet Italian sausages, casings removed, mashed into small pieces
- 2 cups fresh basil, chopped
- 2 cups fresh bread crumbs from white bread or water challah, crusts removed
- 1 medium onion, chopped
- 5 cloves garlic, minced
- 1½ tablespoons fresh oregano, chopped
- 2 teaspoons salt
- 1 teaspoon freshly ground black pepper
- ½ cup tomato sauce
- 3 large eggs, beaten
- ½ cup dry red wine
- ½ cup tomato paste
- 1 teaspoon brown sugar

Prep: Preheat oven to 375°. Grease a large loaf pan lightly with cooking spray. Combine ground beef, zucchini, sausages, basil, bread crumbs, onion, garlic, oregano, salt and pepper in a large bowl. Gently mix in tomato sauce, eggs and wine. Place meat mixture into the prepared loaf pan. Combine tomato paste with brown sugar in a small bowl and brush mixture over meat loaf.

Bake: Bake meat loaf uncovered until cooked through, about 1 hour, 15 minutes. Slice and serve.

plan ahead
Sauce can be prepared a day ahead. Cover and refrigerate.

cook's note
This can be easily prepared overnight if timed properly – put it in to slow-roast before bedtime and take it out when you wake up (omit basting).

pulled brisket sandwiches

North Carolina is famous for its pulled beef BBQ sandwiches, doused with a vinegary sauce. Here is an adapted kosher version, slow cooked to perfection in a crock pot. The texture of brisket works beautifully - it's easy to pull into shreds once tender.

- 2 tablespoons vegetable oil
- 1 (8-pound) first-cut or flat-cut brisket, cut into 3 large pieces
- Kosher salt and freshly ground black pepper, to taste
- 6 cloves garlic, crushed
- 2 cups cream soda
- 4 stalks celery, cut into large pieces
- ⅔ cup packed dark brown sugar
- ½ cup tomato paste
- ½ cup red wine vinegar
- ⅓ cup Dijon mustard
- ⅓ cup soy sauce
- 2 bay leaves
- 1 teaspoon paprika
- 2 loaves French bread or baguettes, cut in half, split lengthwise and toasted

Brown: Heat the vegetable oil in a large skillet over medium-high heat. Season brisket pieces with salt and pepper. Place in the skillet and brown on all sides, about 10 minutes, adding garlic for the last 2 minutes. Transfer the meat and garlic to a 5- to 6-quart crock pot. Pour the soda into the skillet and simmer 30 seconds, scraping up browned bits from the pan; add soda mixture to the crock pot.

Slow Cook: Nestle celery around the meat and add brown sugar, tomato paste, vinegar, mustard, soy sauce, bay leaves and paprika. Stir, then cover and cook on low for 8 hours or on high for 6 hours. Transfer meat to a cutting board and let rest 10 minutes. Using a fork or your fingers, carefully pull the meat apart by its natural striations into thin strips. Serve piled on French bread or baguette and douse with plenty of sauce.

Serving Option: May also be served as an entrée. Simply omit the rolls and pile meat into a deep serving dish; pour sauce over meat.

crispy salami and avocado salad with chicken breast

A meat-lover's dream salad! Crispy spiced salami adds a nice kick and great texture to this satisfying meal-in-one.

prep time
15 minutes

cook time
15-20 minutes

serves
6-8

- ½ teaspoon olive oil
- 12 slices spicy salami (about ⅓ pound), cut into strips
- 1 cooked whole boneless chicken breast, sliced into thin strips
- 2 avocados, peeled, pitted and cut into ½-inch cubes
- ½ pint grape tomatoes, halved
- 1 head romaine hearts, cut into small pieces
- 1 bag (about 4 cups) baby spinach
- Citrus-Curry Dressing *(recipe below)*

plan ahead

Dressing can be made up to 2 days ahead and stored in a tightly sealed container in the refrigerator.

Fry: In a large skillet, heat oil over medium heat. Add salami and fry until crisp, about 15-20 minutes. Transfer to a paper towel-lined plate to remove excess oil.

Assembly: In a large bowl, combine all salad ingredients. Drizzle with Citrus-Curry Dressing, toss and serve.

citrus-curry dressing

- 3 tablespoons lemon juice
- 1 tablespoon orange juice
- 1 tablespoon prepared deli mustard
- 1 teaspoon curry powder
- ½ teaspoon salt
- ¼ teaspoon pepper
- ½ cup olive oil

Combine all ingredients, except oil, in a medium bowl and whisk to blend. Slowly pour in oil in a constant stream, whisking vigorously as oil is added. Continue to whisk until completely blended.

prep time
10 minutes

cook time
15 minutes
for veal,
15 minutes
for jam

serves
2

the prime grill's
porcini rubbed veal chop

CONTRIBUTED BY CHEF DAVID OF THE PRIME GRILL RESTAURANT IN NEW YORK CITY

Prime Grill's Chef David prepares these succulent veal chops to perfection. Now you can experience the restaurant dish at home too!

- 1 double cut veal chop
- 1 tablespoon canola oil

porcini dry rub
- ½ tablespoon black pepper
- 2 tablespoons sugar
- 2 tablespoons kosher salt
- 5 tablespoons "Porcini Pepper" (dried porcini mushrooms ground in spice/coffee grinder)

Prep: Preheat oven to 350°. Combine all of the ingredients of the dry rub in a small bowl. Sprinkle the rub generously on the veal chop before searing.

Cook: Heat oil in a sauté pan over high heat, then place the veal chop in the pan and sear (brown) the veal chop on all sides. Transfer to an oven-ready tray. Roast for approximately 10-15 minutes.

Serve: Remove from oven and serve immediately with Red Pepper Jam (recipe below) and sweet potato soufflé (recipe below).

red pepper jam

- 2 red bell peppers, seeded, ribs out, julienned
- ¼ cup sugar
- ⅓ cup rice vinegar (white vinegar can also be substituted)

Combine all ingredients in a small pot. Bring to a simmer. Slowly cook down until a jam like consistency (almost dry), about 15 minutes.

sweet potato soufflé

- 4 medium sweet potatoes
- ⅓ cup sugar
- Pinch of salt
- 3 eggs
- ½ cup pineapple juice
- 1 vanilla bean, split lengthwise
- ½ cup flour

prep time
5-10 minutes

cook time
40-45 minutes

serves
2-4

Puree: Preheat oven to 400°. Place sweet potatoes in a baking dish and roast uncovered for 1 hour, 15 minutes or until sweet potatoes begin to bubble and skin is crisp. When cool, scoop out sweet potato flesh and puree in a food processor.

Prep: Preheat oven to 325°. Grease a glass baking dish. Combine the first 5 ingredients in a large mixing bowl. Using the tip of a paring knife, gently scrape the seeds from the vanilla bean into the sweet potato puree. Stir to blend and fold in the flour. Pour into the prepared baking dish and cover with foil.

Bake: Place the pan in the oven and bake for approximately 40-45 minutes.

simple tangy skirt steak

Sweet and sour contrasts complement skirt steak beautifully in this easy 1-2-3 dish.

- 1 ⅔ cups (14 ounces) bottled barbecue sauce
- ⅓ cup brown sugar
- ¼ cup lemon juice
- 2 (1-1½ pound) skirt steaks

Prep: Preheat oven to 375°. In a medium bowl, combine BBQ sauce, brown sugar and lemon juice, and mix well.

Bake: Place skirt steak in a glass baking dish slightly larger than the steak itself. Pour sauce over steak and cover tightly. Bake 1 hour, 15 minutes. Slice into 4 large portions and serve.

Serving Option: Steak can be sliced into thin pieces for delicious steak sandwiches. Serve on club or Kaiser rolls.

prep time
5 minutes

cook time
1 hour,
15 minutes

serves
4

This dish freezes beautifully. If making ahead, remove layer of congealed fat before serving.

coffee cajun rubbed ny strip steak

CONTRIBUTED BY AVI PIFKO, GRILLING EXPERT AND AFICIONADO

Coffee lends a beautiful deep flavor that brings out the boldness of the steak and perks up your meal!

- 4 tablespoons bold espresso beans, **ground**
- 1¼ tablespoons freshly ground black pepper
- 1 tablespoon lemon pepper
- ½ teaspoon Cajun seasoning or cayenne pepper
- 1 tablespoon ground cumin
- Olive oil, for brushing
- 2 Shell strip steaks, **1-inch thick (may also be called kosher NY strip steaks)**

Prep: In a small bowl, mix first 5 ingredients to create a dry rub. Lightly brush steaks with oil and season liberally with dry rub.

Grill: Preheat grill to high. Grill steaks for approximately 4 minutes per side, turning only once, for medium-rare; grill 6 minutes per side for medium doneness. Remove steaks from the grill and let rest for 5 minutes before serving.

prep time
5 minutes
cook time
8-10 minutes
serves
2

plan ahead

Dry rub can be prepared ahead and stored in a tightly closed container up to 2 months.

kosher note

This recipe also works beautifully on a boneless fillet steak and a rib eye steak.

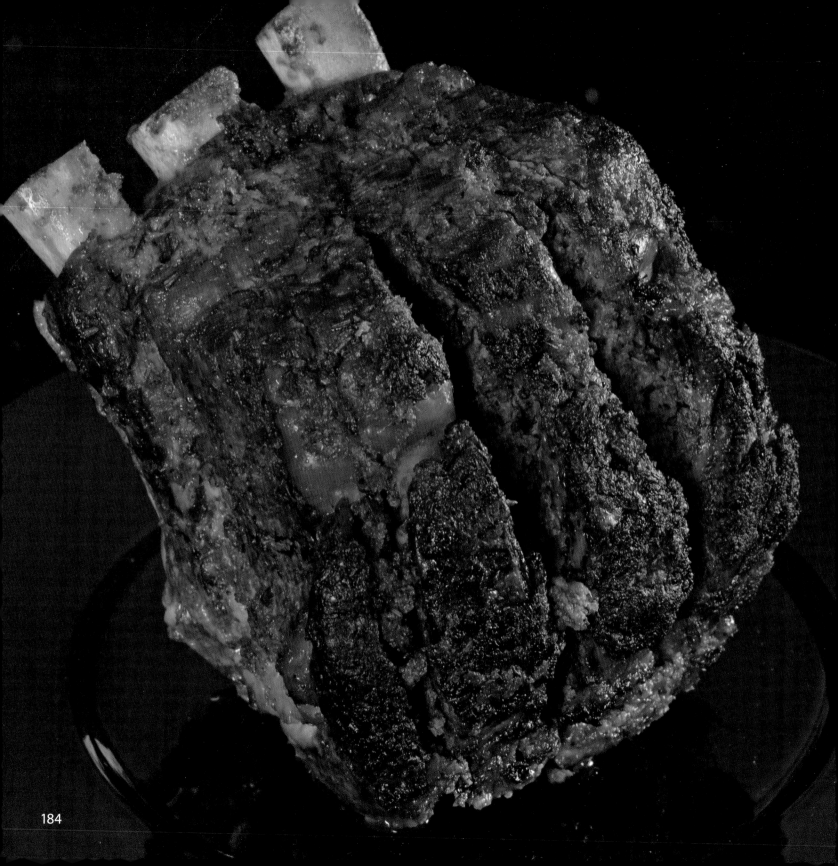

garlic herb crusted rib roast

A standing rib roast is a prime cut of meat from the rib section, bone-in. Its well-marbled meat makes it ideal for dry roasting, leaving a delectable caramelized crust on the exterior, but keeping it juicy and moist on the inside.

prep time
15 minutes

cook time
2 hours,
30 minutes

serves
6-8

- 1 large carrot, peeled
- 2 celery stalks
- 1 large onion, quartered
- 10 cloves garlic, peeled
- ¼ cup olive oil
- 3 tablespoons flour
- 2 tablespoons fresh rosemary, chopped
- 2 tablespoons fresh thyme, chopped
- 2 tablespoons fresh oregano, chopped
- 1 tablespoon salt
- 1½ teaspoons black pepper
- 1 (2-pound) standing rib roast

plan ahead

Herb paste can be made a day ahead and stored in a tightly sealed container in the refrigerator.

cook's note

Increase cooking time for a larger roast, approximately 20 minutes for each additional pound.

Prep: Pureé all ingredients, except roast, in a food processor until they form a paste. Place meat in a roasting pan. Cut 3 deep slices in the top of the roast and fill each with 1½ teaspoons of herb paste. Rub the remainder over the top and sides of roast, covering completely. Let stand for 1 hour at room temperature.

Roast: Preheat oven to 500°. Roast uncovered for 20 minutes. Reduce temperature to 375°. Continue roasting meat until meat thermometer inserted into center registers 130° for medium-rare, about 1 hour, 45 minutes longer; or continue to roast until thermometer reaches 145° for medium, 160° for well-done.

Rest: Remove meat from oven and let stand for 20 minutes (temperature will continue to rise 15°-20° while resting). Slice before serving.

Serving Option: This roast can also be made as a boneless roast—reduce cooking time by 25 minutes and use a meat thermometer to check for doneness.

sides

couscous with dates, olives and mint

Healthy and flavorful, this Mediterranean-inspired dish is a delicious complement for any fish dish and wonderful to savor all on its own.

prep time
10 minutes

cook time
15 minutes

serves
6

- 2 cups vegetable broth
- 1 teaspoon kosher salt, plus more to taste
- 1½ tablespoons extra-virgin olive oil
- 1 (10-ounce) package plain couscous (about 1⅔ cups)
- 1 (15-ounce) can chickpeas, undrained
- 12 large green olives, pitted, quartered lengthwise
- 6 Medjool dates, pitted and diced
- 2 teaspoons fresh lemon juice (from ½ lemon)
- ¼ cup chopped fresh mint leaves
- Freshly ground black pepper, to taste
- ¼ cup feta cheese, crumbled

Couscous: Bring broth, salt and oil to a boil in a small saucepan over medium-high heat. Slowly mix in couscous, cover and remove from heat. Let stand 15 minutes. Gently fluff couscous with a fork. Set aside.

Chickpeas: Place chickpeas with their canning liquid in a small saucepan. Bring to a boil over medium heat and reduce heat to medium-low, simmering until chickpeas are heated through, about 3 minutes, and drain.

Assemble: Combine couscous, chickpeas, olives, dates, lemon juice and mint in a large bowl. Stir to incorporate evenly. Season with salt and pepper. Top with crumbled feta cheese.

Serving Option: For a light and healthy lunch option, toss chopped romaine lettuce with lemon juice, olive oil, salt and pepper. Transfer to a large plate, and then mound couscous on top of the lettuce. Sprinkle with feta cheese and enjoy!

art deco vegetable tart

Vibrant, beautiful colors and patterns make this tart stand out on your table. With the addition of fresh herbs, it tastes as good as it looks!

- 3 tablespoons coarsely chopped fresh flat-leaf parsley
- 2 tablespoons coarsely chopped fresh oregano
- 1 tablespoon coarsely chopped fresh thyme
- 1 clove garlic, minced
- ¼ cup extra-virgin olive oil, divided
- Kosher salt and freshly ground black pepper, to taste
- 2 small zucchini, unpeeled and cut into ⅛-inch-thick rounds
- 2 small yellow squash, unpeeled and cut into ⅛-inch-thick rounds
- 2 plum tomatoes, cut into ⅛-inch thick rounds
- ½ cup honey mustard
- 2 teaspoons soy sauce
- 1 (12x17-inch) puff pastry sheet, defrosted
- ½ cup pitted Kalamata olives, chopped

garnish
- Fresh basil leaves, chopped

Prep: Preheat oven to 400°. In a small bowl, combine parsley, oregano, thyme, garlic and 3 tablespoons oil; season with salt and pepper. Set aside. In a separate bowl, combine zucchini, yellow squash and plum tomatoes with 1 tablespoon oil; season with salt and pepper. Set aside. In a third small bowl, combine the honey mustard with soy sauce.

Assembly: Roll out puff pastry on floured surface to 11x13-inch rectangle. Fold the edges inwards by ¾ inch, pressing to adhere. Transfer to a rimmed baking sheet. Pierce surface evenly with a fork, avoiding folded edges. Brush honey mustard mixture evenly over crust within folded edges. Arrange vegetable rounds atop honey mustard, overlapping slightly. Drizzle herb and garlic mixture over the vegetables; top with olives.

Bake: Bake until edges are browned, about 30-35 minutes. Let cool slightly. Cut into 6 squares; garnish with basil.

Dairy Serving Option: Sprinkle ½ cup crumbled feta cheese over the tart immediately before baking.

asparagus in creamy hazelnut sauce

Real butter. Pure decadence…and no leftovers.

- 1 package large garlic croutons
- ¼ cup hazelnuts, **toasted and chopped**
- 2 tablespoons hazelnut oil or peanut oil
- Kosher salt and freshly ground black pepper, **to taste**
- 16-20 large asparagus spears (about 1½ pounds), **woody ends trimmed**
- 1 stick (½ cup) unsalted butter
- 2 egg yolks
- 1 tablespoon water
- 2 teaspoons fresh lemon juice (from ½ lemon)
- 2 cloves garlic
- ¼ teaspoon nutmeg

Croutons: Place croutons and hazelnuts in a zip top bag and pound with the back of a skillet or mallet to break the cubes into large, uneven crumbs. Mix in oil and season with freshly ground black pepper. Set aside.

Asparagus: Add a dash of salt to water in a large saucepan and bring water to a boil. When water boils, add the asparagus. Bring water back to a boil, cover and cook for 3 minutes (the asparagus should be tender but crisp). Remove from heat, drain and spread the spears on a tray to cool.

Hazelnut sauce: Melt butter in a saucepan. As the butter melts and foams, some solids will stick to the bottom of the pan, turning a light brown color. Remove from heat and allow butter to cool for 5 minutes. Combine egg yolks and water in a blender, and while the blender is running, slowly add the butter. Add lemon juice, garlic and nutmeg to the mixture. Season to taste with salt and pepper. Blend for a few more seconds. The mixture should be smooth and creamy.

Serve: If necessary, reheat the asparagus in a microwave for about 1 minute or warm in the oven for a few minutes at 180°. Drizzle sauce over asparagus and top with a generous sprinkling of the hazelnut-crouton mixture. Serve immediately.

prep time
25 minutes

cook time
1 hour,
35 minutes

serves
8

spanish potato galette

For all those potato lovers out there, here's another great way to enjoy this all time favorite.

- 6 cups potatoes, peeled and thinly sliced (about 3 pounds)
- 2 cups sweet onions (such as Vidalia or Maui), thinly sliced
- 2 tablespoons olive oil, divided
- 2 teaspoons kosher salt, divided
- 4 large eggs
- 1 tablespoon fresh oregano, chopped, plus more for garnish
- ¼ cup black olives, pitted & sliced (optional)

Potatoes: Preheat oven to 375°. Place potatoes and onions in a large greased baking dish. Drizzle with 1 tablespoon plus 2 teaspoons oil and sprinkle with 1½ teaspoons salt. Toss well. Bake for 1 hour, 20 minutes or until potatoes are tender, stirring occasionally to prevent sticking.

Prepare galette: Combine eggs, remaining ½ teaspoon salt and oregano in a large bowl. Stir in potato mixture & olives. Let stand for 10 minutes. Heat remaining teaspoon of oil in a large skillet over medium heat. Pour potato mixture into pan. Cook for 8-10 minutes or until almost set, shaking pan frequently.

Flip: Place a plate upside down on top of pan. Invert galette onto plate. Carefully slide the galette, cooked-side up, back into pan. Cook for another 3 minutes or until set, occasionally shaking the pan gently. Carefully loosen with a spatula and slide onto a plate. Cool and cut into wedges. Garnish with fresh oregano.

warm asian rice stir fry

This hearty side dish can also be served as a vegetarian main course.

prep time
15-20 minutes

cook time
15-20 minutes

serves
4

plan ahead
Vegetables can
be prepped a
day ahead.

- ½ cup water, divided
- ¼ cup soy sauce
- 2 teaspoons cornstarch
- 1 teaspoon honey
- 1 tablespoon fresh ginger, grated
- 2 tablespoons peanut oil
- 1 medium onion, peeled and sliced
- 1 small red bell pepper, cut into thin strips
- 1 clove garlic, minced
- 1 cup broccoli florets (about 6 ounces)
- 1 (6-ounce) package portabella mushroom caps, stems removed, dark gills scraped and cut into ¾-inch pieces
- 1 romaine heart or 1 bunch baby bok choy, cut into long thin strips
- 1 cup cooked basmati white rice (warmed)
- Freshly ground black pepper, to taste

garnish
- ½ cup pecan halves, toasted and chopped
- ¼ cup thinly sliced scallions

Sauce: Combine ¼ cup water, soy sauce, cornstarch, honey and ginger in a small bowl. Whisk to blend. Set aside.

Cook: Heat oil in a wok (or a large skillet with cover) over medium-high heat. Add onion, bell pepper and garlic; cook and stir for 3 minutes. Add broccoli and mushrooms, and stir for 1 minute to combine. Add remaining ¼ cup water; cover and cook for 3-5 minutes or until vegetables are crisp yet tender. Add sauce, stirring for 2-3 minutes or until bubbly and thickened. Remove from heat. Immediately add the chopped romaine or bok choy and toss to combine.

Assembly: Combine warm rice with vegetables. Season to taste with freshly ground black pepper. Serve warm, topped with a sprinkling of pecans and scallions.

pastrami stuffed onions

A pastrami-studded stuffing is the star of this attractive side dish, but leftover stuffing can be served on its own or frozen and reserved for another time.

prep time
55 minutes

cook time
1 hour,
15 minutes

serves
8

- 8 large white or yellow onions, evenly sized, unpeeled
- ½ cup water
- 2 tablespoons canola oil
- 1 pound pastrami, diced
- 3 celery stalks, diced
- 1 teaspoon salt
- 1 teaspoon freshly ground black pepper
- 3 cloves garlic, minced
- 15 ounces baby spinach, stems trimmed and coarsely chopped (14 cups)
- 1 small water challah or 3 water challah rolls, cut into ½-inch cubes (10 cups), lightly toasted
- 1 cup chicken stock

Onions: Preheat oven to 425°. Slice off a ½-inch-thick layer from the tops of the unpeeled onions, discarding tops, and trim just enough from the bottoms for the onions to stand upright. Using a small spoon, scoop out all but the outer 2 or 3 layers from each onion, being careful not to puncture through the bottom. Coarsely chop 3 cups of the scooped-out onion and set aside. Arrange onion shells (hollow ends up) in a large roasting pan. Add ½ cup water to the bottom of the pan and cover tightly with foil. Roast onions in the middle of oven until tender but still intact, about 30-35 minutes.

Stuffing: Heat oil in a large skillet over medium-high heat. Add reserved chopped onion, pastrami, celery, salt and pepper. Sauté, stirring often until vegetables are softened, about 5 minutes. Add garlic and sauté for another 1-2 minutes. Transfer mixture to a large bowl and stir in spinach, challah and stock. Cool completely.

Bake: Reduce oven temperature to 350°. Transfer onion shells to a work surface and discard water in pan. Fill shells with stuffing, mounding it in the center, and return them to the pan. Bake uncovered in the center of the oven until heated through, about 25 minutes.

string beans with lemon zest

Bright and crisp, this no-fuss dish yields extraordinary results where the freshest ingredients are showcased.

plan ahead

Green beans can be prepared and refrigerated a day ahead. Bring to room temperature before serving.

- 2½ teaspoons kosher salt, **divided**
- 1 pound string beans **trimmed**
- 2 tablespoons extra-virgin olive oil
- Zest (peel) of 1 medium lemon

- 1 tablespoon fresh lemon juice
- 1 clove garlic, **minced**
- Freshly ground black pepper, **to taste**

Boil: Fill a large saucepan with water and 2 teaspoons salt. Bring to a boil over high heat. Add the string beans and boil for up to 5 minutes-the string beans will turn bright green. Immediately remove from heat, drain in a colander and run under very cold water to halt the cooking process.

Dress: Combine oil, zest, lemon juice, garlic, remaining ½ teaspoon salt and pepper in a large bowl. Whisk to blend. Add green beans to the bowl, tossing to coat with dressing. Serve at room temperature.

cauliflower with smoked paprika, almonds and garlic

Spice up your cauliflower with fresh aromatics! A little bit of high-quality paprika goes a long way.

prep time
10 minutes

cook time
20 minutes

serves
8

- 3 tablespoons extra-virgin olive oil, **divided**
- 6 cloves garlic, **unpeeled**
- ½ cup whole almonds, **coarsely chopped**
- 3 large cloves garlic, **peeled and chopped**
- 1½ teaspoons smoked paprika
- Kosher salt and freshly ground black pepper, **to taste**
- 2 heads cauliflower, **separated into small florets**
- ⅓ cup water
- 1-2 teaspoons sherry wine vinegar

Sauté: Heat 1 tablespoon oil in a heavy large skillet over medium-high heat. Add whole cloves garlic and sauté until slightly soft, about 6 minutes. Add almonds. Stir until lightly browned, another 2-3 minutes. Add chopped garlic and paprika. Season with salt and pepper; sauté 1 more minute. Transfer mixture to a small bowl.

Steam: Add remaining 2 tablespoons oil to the skillet and return skillet to medium-high heat. Add cauliflower; season with salt and pepper. Add water; cover and steam until cauliflower is crisp yet tender, about 6 minutes. Drain off and discard any water from skillet. Stir in almond mixture (whole cloves garlic can be left in or discarded as desired). Season with additional salt and pepper, if necessary. Mix in vinegar. Transfer cauliflower to serving bowl and serve.

herb stuffed mushrooms

Here is a great way to change things up a bit and take mushrooms to the next level. These mushrooms are best made and served fresh. Look for mushrooms that are unblemished and have no odor.

prep time
15 minutes

cook time
30 minutes

serves
8-10

- 24 (1½-2-inch-wide) baby bella mushrooms with stems or 10 large portabella caps
- 2 tablespoons olive oil
- 1 large clove garlic, minced
- 1½ teaspoons fresh oregano, finely chopped
- 1 teaspoon fresh cilantro, minced
- 4 ounces pecans (about 1 cup), finely chopped
- ½ teaspoon nutmeg
- ¾ teaspoon salt, divided
- ¼ teaspoon black pepper, divided
- ⅔ cup milk or plain soy milk, divided

cook's note

For a nut-free option, substitute pecans with ½ cup panko bread crumbs.

Prep: Preheat oven to 375°. Carefully remove stems from the mushrooms, leaving the caps intact. Finely chop stems and set aside. Arrange the caps, stem side up, in a lightly greased 9x13-inch baking dish.

Sauté: In a medium skillet, heat oil over medium heat. Add chopped mushroom stems, garlic, oregano and cilantro and sauté, stirring frequently, until lightly browned, about 3-5 minutes. Stir in pecans, nutmeg, ½ teaspoon salt and ⅛ teaspoon pepper. Cook, stirring frequently, for about 1 more minute. Stir in ⅓ cup milk or soy milk and bring to a simmer; then remove from heat.

Bake: Season insides of mushroom caps with remaining salt and pepper, and then divide filling among the caps. Drizzle mushrooms with remaining ⅓ cup milk or soy milk and bake until filling is browned and caps are tender, about 30 minutes. Serve mushrooms drizzled with pan juices.

Dairy Option: For a delicious crusty finish, sprinkle a layer of freshly grated parmesan cheese over the tops of the mushrooms before baking.

prep time
45 minutes plus
3 hours soaking
time

cook time
1 hour,
45 minutes

serves
8

plan ahead

*Dish can be
prepared until this
point up to
2 days in advance.
Cover and
refrigerate until
baking time.*

cook's note

*Sausage is easier to
cut when frozen.*

*If bread is fresh, the
cut bread
can be left out
on the counter
to dry out for
up to 6 hours.*

smoky apple chestnut bread pudding

When savory stuffing meets sweet bread pudding, the results are quite satisfying. Serve as an accompaniment to turkey or duck.

bread mixture
- 2 cups plain soy milk
- 4 large eggs
- 2 teaspoons onion powder
- 1½ teaspoons kosher salt
- ½ teaspoon freshly ground black pepper
- ½ tablespoon fresh sage, finely chopped
- 2 tablespoons fresh parsley, chopped
- 3 cups ½-inch-cubed day-old challah or white bread

filling
- 2 tablespoons extra-virgin olive oil
- 6 Italian veal sausages (preferably smoky apple flavor), cubed or cut into ½-inch rounds
- 2 cups onions (2 small or 1 large onion), chopped
- 1 pound granny smith apples, peeled, cored and cubed (about 3⅓ cups)
- 2 cups (about 14 ounces) jarred peeled whole chestnuts
- 4 teaspoons fresh thyme, chopped
- 2 tablespoons brown sugar
- Kosher salt and freshly ground black pepper, to taste
- 1 cup dry red wine
- 1 cup low-sodium chicken broth
- 1 cup pitted prunes (packed), chopped

Bread Mixture: Mix soy milk, eggs, onion powder, salt, pepper, sage and parsley in a large bowl to blend. Add cubed bread and stir to coat. Cover and refrigerate until bread absorbs liquid, at least 3 hours.

Filling: Preheat oven to 400°. Heat oil in a large skillet over medium-high heat. Add sausages and sauté until edges are crisp, about 9 minutes. Add onions and sauté until lightly browned, about 12 minutes. Add apples, chestnuts, thyme and brown sugar. Season with salt and pepper. Sauté for 5 minutes to blend flavors. Add red wine. Bring back to a boil until thick and syrupy, about 2 minutes. Add broth and simmer uncovered for another 10 minutes to reduce the liquid. Spread mixture in a 9x13-inch oven-safe casserole dish and bake uncovered until apples are tender, about 20 minutes. Remove from oven. Mix in prunes and season with additional salt and pepper, if necessary.*

Bake: Reduce oven temperature to 325°. Spread bread mixture evenly over filling. Bake until puffed, browned and firm, about 50 minutes.

potatoes gremolata

A gremolata is a mixture made of minced parsley, lemon zest and garlic that can be used as a garnish to finish a dish or as a topping that accentuates and brings out flavor. Roasted potatoes get a "new look" with this enticing combo.

prep time
15 minutes

cook time
1 hour,
25 minutes

serves
6

- 2 pounds baby or fingerling potatoes
- ¼ cup olive oil
- 6 cloves garlic, unpeeled
- 3 cloves garlic, minced

gremolata
- 3 tablespoons extra-virgin olive oil
- Zest of 2 lemons
- 3 tablespoons fresh lemon juice (from 2 lemons)
- 2 tablespoons fresh parsley leaves, chopped
- 1 tablespoon fresh thyme leaves, chopped
- Kosher salt and freshly ground black pepper, to taste

plan ahead

Potatoes can be boiled a day ahead. Cover and refrigerate until roasting time.

Potatoes: Preheat oven to 400°. Place potatoes in an 8-quart stockpot with enough cold water to cover by at least 2 inches. Bring the water to a boil over medium heat and cook until potatoes are tender when pierced with a fork, about 25 minutes. Drain and allow to dry for 5 minutes.

Roast: Place potatoes in a roasting pan. Add oil, whole garlic cloves and minced garlic. Bake for 45 minutes. Meanwhile, combine all ingredients for gremolata in a small bowl. Sprinkle potatoes with gremolata and toss to evenly coat potatoes. Return to oven and bake uncovered for another 15–20 minutes. Transfer to a serving bowl and serve.

simplify

Canned pineapple
(drained) and
frozen cranberries
can be used
instead of fresh.

pineapple cranberry crisp

The bright fresh flavor of cranberries combined with the tangy sweetness of fresh pineapple is irresistible. The crispy topping only adds to the dish's infectious flavor.

topping
- 1 cup dark brown sugar (packed)
- ¾ cup flour
- 1 cup old fashioned oats
- 1 cup chopped pecans
- ½ cup (1 stick) margarine, cubed, room temperature

filling
- ½ cup sugar
- ¼ cup flour
- ½ teaspoon ground cinnamon
- ¼ teaspoon ground allspice
- 2 Golden Delicious apples, peeled and cubed
- 1 green apple, peeled and cubed
- 2 cups fresh cranberries
- 2 cups (½-inch) cubed fresh pineapple

Prep: Preheat oven to 375°. Grease a 9x13-inch baking dish.

Topping: Combine brown sugar, flour, oats and pecans in a medium bowl. Add margarine. Using your fingertips, blend mixture until coarse crumbs form. Set aside.

Filling: Whisk together sugar, flour, cinnamon and allspice in a large bowl. Add apples, cranberries and pineapple. Stir until evenly mixed.

Bake: Transfer filling to prepared baking dish. Sprinkle topping evenly over filling. Bake until filling is bubbling and topping is brown and crisp, about 40 minutes. Cool at least 15 minutes before serving.

spiced fruity challah kugel

Sweet white wine macerates chunks of fruit that stud this sweet, spiced challah kugel, adding a new dimension to bread pudding.

- 1 cup raisins
- 1 cups white dessert wine
- 2 cups milk or soy milk (not low fat)
- ½ cup orange juice
- 1 teaspoon vanilla extract
- 1½ teaspoons cinnamon
- ¼ teaspoon salt
- 3 large eggs, beaten
- 3 cups cubed water challah or other white bread
- Zest of 1 lemon
- ½ cup chopped dates
- 2 ripe medium pears, peeled, cored and cubed
- 1 large Golden Delicious apple, peeled, cored and cubed
- 1½ cups sugar

prep time
15 minutes plus soaking times

cook time
1 hour

serves
8-10

plan ahead

Kugel can be prepared 2 days ahead. It also freezes well.

cook's note

Challah kugel (and bread puddings in general) benefit from using very dry bread that absorbs custard without getting soggy.

Prep: Place oven rack on middle shelf and put a sheet of foil on bottom rack to catch any drips. Preheat oven to 400°. Spray bottom and sides of a 10-inch round springform pan with cooking spray.

Soak: Place raisins in a small bowl and add wine. Soak until raisins are plumped, about 1 hour.

Bread mixture: Combine milk or soy milk, orange juice, vanilla, cinnamon, salt and eggs in a large bowl. Whisk to blend and add challah or bread. Soak for at least 10 minutes (or up to 1 hour). Add raisin mixture, lemon zest, dates, pears, apple and sugar. Gently mix and pour into the prepared pan.

Bake: Bake until golden and evenly set, 50-60 minutes, until golden brown. Cool completely in the pan on a rack, 1-2 hours, then refrigerate covered for 4 hours for flavors to develop. Heat before serving or bring to room temperature. Using a knife, loosen the kugel from the edges of the pan and remove springform sides.

quinoa with balsamic roasted vegetables

prep time
20-25 minutes

cook time
40-45 minutes

serves
8

A South American staple grain, quinoa (KEEN-WAH) is now considered the "supergrain of the future," boasting more protein than any other grain, as well as all 8 essential amino acids. With its high nutritive value, quinoa is also an optimal choice for those following a gluten-free diet.

- 3 tablespoons extra-virgin olive oil
- 2 cloves garlic, minced
- ½ tablespoon brown sugar
- 1 tablespoon Herbs de Provence
- 1 tablespoon balsamic vinegar
- Kosher salt and freshly ground black pepper, to taste
- 1 red pepper, cut into 1-inch squares
- 1 yellow pepper, cut into 1-inch squares
- 1 red onion, halved and sliced ¼-inch-thick
- 1 Vidalia onion, halved and sliced ¼-inch-thick
- 1 portabella mushroom, sliced into ½-inch-thick pieces
- 1 zucchini, sliced into ½-inch-thick semicircles
- 1 yellow squash, sliced into ½-inch-thick semicircles
- 1¾ cups low-sodium chicken broth
- 2 cups quinoa, rinsed and drained

Roast: Preheat oven to 400°. In a large bowl, combine oil, garlic, brown sugar, Herbs de Provence and vinegar. Season liberally with salt and pepper. Whisk to blend. Add peppers, onions, mushrooms, zucchini and squash. Toss to coat vegetables. Spread mixture onto 2 greased cookie sheets in a single layer. Roast for 40-45 minutes.

Quinoa: While vegetables are roasting, prepare quinoa. Place stock in a medium saucepan. Add quinoa and bring to a boil. Cover, reduce flame to low and continue to simmer until all liquid is absorbed, about 10-15 minutes or until quinoa appears translucent (with the germ ring visible around its edge). Fluff quinoa with a fork, add vegetables and gently toss together. Season with more salt and pepper, if necessary.

prep time
15 minutes

cook time
1 hour,
15 minutes

serves
8

plan ahead
Wild rice can be prepared a day ahead. Cover and refrigerate.

coconut jasmine rice

Sweet coconut and pineapple give a vibrant Asian spin to this simple rice accompaniment.

- 5½ cups water, **divided**
- 1 cup wild rice or long grain black rice
- 1½ teaspoons salt, **divided**
- 2 tablespoons olive oil
- 2 cups jasmine white rice

- 1 (14-ounce) can unsweetened coconut milk
- ¼ cup dried sweetened flaked coconut
- 3 tablespoons sugar
- 1 cup cubed fresh or canned pineapple
- Freshly ground black pepper, **to taste**

Wild rice: Bring 4 cups water to a boil in a medium saucepan. Add wild rice and ½ teaspoon salt; return to a boil. Reduce heat to low, cover and simmer until tender, about 50 minutes. Drain excess water.

White rice: Heat oil in a large heavy saucepan over medium-high heat. Add jasmine rice and stir for 2 minutes. Add remaining 1½ cups water, 1 teaspoon salt, coconut milk, coconut and sugar. Bring to a boil. Add pineapple, cover and reduce heat to low. Cook until rice is tender, about 15 minutes. Stir in wild rice. Season to taste with salt and pepper.

garlicky string beans with sun-dried tomatoes

Served warm or cold, these zesty flavors complement grilled meats nicely.

prep time
15 minutes
cook time
3-5 minutes
serves
6

- 1 pound string beans, **trimmed**
- ½ cup sun-dried tomatoes packed in oil, **drained and thinly sliced**
- 1 small red onion, **thinly sliced**
- ¼ cup toasted pine nuts

basil-garlic dressing

- 2 cloves garlic
- ¼ cup red wine vinegar
- 2 teaspoons salt
- 2 tablespoons Dijon mustard
- 1 tablespoon sugar
- ½ cup extra-virgin olive oil
- 15 basil leaves
- Freshly ground black pepper, **to taste**

plan ahead

Dressing can be prepared up to 2 days in advance. Store in a tightly covered container and refrigerate.

Prep: Place all dressing ingredients in a food processor. Process until mixture is blended and smooth.

Steam: Fill a medium saucepan with 1-2 inches of water. Bring to a boil over medium-high heat. Place a steamer basket over the water and add string beans. Cover and steam until they turn bright green (are tender but still crisp), about 3-5 minutes. Remove from heat and quickly immerse string beans in ice cold water to halt the cooking process.

Assembly: Combine string beans, sun-dried tomatoes, onion and pine nuts in a large serving bowl. Dress with Basil-Garlic Dressing immediately before serving; toss gently to combine.

balsamic cipollini onions

Cipollini onions are "little onions" in Italian. They are about the size of a slightly flattened golf ball. With their thin skin and high sugar content, they are ideal for caramelizing, and perfectly balanced by the acidity of the vinegar in this show-stopping recipe! Cipollinis are a great complement for meats and roasts…or simply perfect on their own.

- 2 pounds cipollini onions, unpeeled
- 1 cup sugar
- ¼ cup water
- 1 cup dry red wine
- 1 cup red wine vinegar
- 2 tablespoons extra-virgin olive oil
- 1 teaspoon salt
- 10 whole black peppercorns
- 1 bay leaf
- 1 tablespoon balsamic vinegar

Blanch: Bring a large pot of water to a rolling boil over high heat. Add onions and cook for 1 minute. Drain and rinse with very cold water. Peel onions, leaving the ends intact.

Cook: Combine sugar and water in a medium saucepan over medium heat. Stir only until sugar is dissolved. Bring to a boil, wiping down the sides of the pot with a wet pastry brush (do not touch the mixture). Do not stir. Keep boiling until mixture turns a pale golden color. Start swirling the pan until color is a deep amber (color will change quickly). Quickly remove from heat and carefully add wine (the steam will explode upwards so be careful). Return the pot to the flame and simmer, stirring until the harden sugar that has formed, has dissolved.

Simmer: Add onions, red wine vinegar, oil, salt, peppercorns and bay leaf. Simmer uncovered for 1 hour, stirring occasionally. Remove onions from liquid and transfer to a serving bowl. Continue to boil liquid until reduced and slightly thickened, approximately 3 minutes. Watch carefully as the liquid can quickly burn. Add balsamic vinegar and pour liquid over onions. Cool to room temperature, and serve.

prep time
10 minutes

cook time
1 hour,
15 minutes

serves
6-8

plan ahead

This dish can be prepared up to 2 weeks in advance. Cover and store in the refrigerator. The flavors deepen with age.

simplify

Use frozen pearl onions when fresh cipollini onions are not available.

rainbow rice dome

Arborio rice is a glutinous short-grain rice – the traditional choice for making risotto, a creamy Italian rice dish. Risotto is slowly cooked on the stovetop by incorporating small amounts of liquid into the grains until they are absorbed.

- ⅓ cup extra-virgin olive oil
- 1 cup minced onion (from 1 medium or 2 small onions)
- 2 cups Arborio rice
- 1 cup dry white wine
- 6 cups vegetable broth
- ⅛ teaspoon saffron
- 2 tablespoons plain soy milk
- 3 egg yolks
- 2 teaspoons onion powder
- 1½ teaspoons salt
- Freshly ground black pepper, to taste
- 1¾ cups frozen chopped spinach, thawed and drained
- 3 tablespoons tomato paste

Risotto Base: Heat oil over medium-high heat in a large deep skillet. Add onion and sauté until translucent, about 5-7 minutes. Add rice and brown, stirring frequently, for 2 minutes. Add wine and continue cooking until liquid evaporates. Add 1 cup of broth, and continue to stir constantly until it is absorbed. Lower the heat to medium-low (a simmer should be maintained) and continue adding broth gradually by ½ cupfuls until rice is cooked through but still firm, about 20 minutes. Dissolve saffron in soy milk and stir into rice. Remove from heat; add egg yolks and onion powder. Season with salt and pepper, and gently stir to blend.

Prep: Preheat the oven to 400°. Grease an 8-inch mold with high sides or an oven-proof glass bowl.

Color: Divide risotto base into 3 equal parts in separate bowls. Add spinach into one part and mix to combine well; add tomato paste into another part and mix to combine well; leave the third part white. Layer white, red and then green risottos into the prepared mold or glass bowl, using a rubber spatula to flatten out each layer. Cover with foil. Tap the mold on the counter to settle the layers.

Bake: Place the mold into a large roasting pan filled halfway with warm water and bake for 20 minutes. Remove from oven and let rest at least 5 minutes. To serve, place a platter upside down on top of the mold and gently flip over to rest on the platter. With a gentle twisting motion, remove the mold. (Do not unmold until ready to serve.)

apple fig crisp

The combination of apples and figs is old world with modern flair. The flavors will linger long after the last bite is finished.

prep time
20 minutes

cook time
1 hour,
20 minutes

serves
8-10

plan ahead
Kugel can be prepared 2 days ahead. It also freezes well.

- 1½ cups sweet red wine
- 1¼ cups water
- ¾ cup sugar
- 3 tablespoons orange juice
- 2 tablespoons fresh lemon juice
- 2 teaspoons apple pie spice
- 1 pound dried figs, **quartered**
- ½ cup apple butter
- 4 tablespoons unsalted butter or olive oil
- 3¼ pounds (about 8-9 medium) Granny Smith apples, **peeled, cored and cut into wedges**
- ½ cup packed brown sugar
- 1 teaspoon ground cinnamon
- ¼ teaspoon nutmeg

crumb topping
- 2¼ cups flour
- ⅓ cup sugar
- 2 tablespoons packed brown sugar
- 1 tablespoon baking powder
- 1 teaspoon salt
- 5 tablespoons chilled unsalted butter or margarine, **cut into pieces**
- 1 cup milk or soy milk
- ½ teaspoon almond extract

Figs: Combine wine, water, sugar, orange juice, lemon juice and apple pie spice in a large, heavy saucepan. Bring to a boil over medium heat and simmer for 20 minutes. Add figs to liquid and simmer over medium heat until figs are tender, about 20 minutes. Drain figs and discard liquid.

Apples: Preheat oven to 350°. Spray a 13x9x2-inch oven-to-table baking dish with cooking spray and spread apple butter over bottom of dish. Melt butter or heat oil in a large, heavy skillet over medium heat. Add apples and sauté until tender, about 10 minutes. Add brown sugar, cinnamon and nutmeg; toss gently to combine. Gently stir in figs. Transfer mixture to the prepared baking dish.

Topping: Combine flour, sugar, brown sugar, baking powder and salt in a large bowl. Add butter or margarine and blend with fingertips until coarse meal forms. Add milk or soy milk and almond extract, stirring with a fork until moist dough forms. Drop dough by the tablespoonful atop fruit in dish.

Bake: Bake until fruit is tender and topping is golden brown, about 25 minutes. Serve hot and bubbling.

dilled zucchini with grape tomatoes

When zucchini abounds in the summer months, prepare this farm-fresh dish.
Simple and delicious, it can be served warm or at room temperature.

- 2 tablespoons extra-virgin olive oil
- 1 small onion, diced
- 4 medium zucchini, peeled and sliced into ¼-inch rounds
- 1 tablespoon honey
- 1 tablespoon lemon juice
- 1 tablespoon beef consommé powder
- 10 grape tomatoes, halved
- 1 small bunch fresh dill, chopped (about ¼ cup)
- Freshly ground black pepper, to taste

Sauté: Heat oil over medium heat in a large skillet. Add onions and sauté until translucent, about 5-7 minutes. Add zucchini and cover, stirring occasionally to keep onions from browning, about 5 more minutes. Zucchini will begin to sweat. Add honey, lemon juice and consommé powder. Stir to blend. Cover and cook for another 5 minutes until zucchini becomes tender. Add tomatoes and dill, stir and cover for 2 more minutes. Season with pepper to taste.

sweet potato crumble in orange cups

Marshmallow-pecan topping on sweet potato pie is a tasty surprise on a classic dish. The flavors are earthy and sweet and will enhance any Thanksgiving table.

prep time
15 minutes

cook time
2 hours

yields
18

sweet potato filling
- 6 pounds large yams (red-skinned sweet potatoes), **unpeeled**
- ¾ cup marshmallow fluff, **plus more** for garnish
- 8 tablespoons margarine, **softened**
- 6 tablespoons maple syrup
- ¼ cup brown sugar
- ⅛ teaspoon salt
- 3 large eggs

streusel topping
- ¾ cup flour
- ¾ cup dark brown sugar
- ½ teaspoon cinnamon
- ½ teaspoon ginger
- ½ cup margarine, **softened**
- ¾ cup quick cooking oats
- ½ cup chopped walnuts
- 9 large oranges

garnish
- 36 pecan halves

plan ahead
Sweet potato filling can be made a day ahead. Cover and refrigerate.

simplify
Substitute yams with 1 can yams in heavy syrup, mashed, and omit the brown sugar.

Filling: Preheat oven to 400°. Place sweet potatoes in a large baking pan. Bake uncovered for 1½-1¾ hours or until a fork pierces easily into the potatoes and the flesh is soft. Remove from oven and let cool. Cut sweet potatoes in half; scoop out pulp into a large bowl. Add ¾ cup marshmallow fluff, margarine, maple syrup, brown sugar and salt. Mash until smooth. Whisk in eggs, stirring to blend.

Topping: Mix flour, brown sugar, cinnamon and ginger in a medium bowl. Add margarine, tossing to blend with a fork until coarse crumbs form. Stir in oats and walnuts.

Bake: Preheat oven to 350°. Cut a thin slice from top and bottom of each orange to make flat surfaces. Cut oranges in half. Scoop out the fruit and pulp (fruit can be reserved for another use). Place orange cups on 2 baking sheets and divide sweet potato mixture equally among them. Sprinkle streusel topping over each cup (there will be leftover topping). For an additional garnish, top each cup with a dollop of marshmallow fluff and 2 pecan halves. Bake until tops begin to brown, about 30 minutes.

Serving option: This recipe can also be prepared as one large sweet potato pie using a deep-dish pie crust. Spread sweet potato filling evenly inside pie crust. Sprinkle with topping and bake for 40 minutes at 350°.

bread & dairy

cheese

A cheese platter is a great option for a starter course or dessert course. Use between 3 to 5 cheeses, to offer an interesting variety. Calculate 3 ounces of cheese per guest for a platter or individual appetizers. Try to select cheeses for your platter that combine styles, textures and colors, and that offer different looks, tastes, and feels. You can feature breads or baguettes and interesting crackers, bread sticks and flat breads together as well. Fruit, like apples, pears, grapes, strawberries and figs, together with assorted nuts, can be included too.

Arrange the platter at least an hour prior to serving so the flavors can fully ripen. Provide a separate knife for each selection so that the flavors don't mingle.

See photo for examples, in clockwise order:

Danish Blue Cheese: Has a bold, pungent flavor and works beautifully crumbled on a cracker with a slice of fresh pear to mellow its flavor.

Syrian Cheese: Is a simple, unripened cheese with a delicate flavor. It is soft, white, smooth, creamy and mild. The cheese tastes delicious spread on fresh bread or a cracker, and paired with sweet fruits like strawberries and figs.

Goat cheese: Is a creamy cheese. It comes in a variety of flavors such as cranberry and blueberry. It is delicious on a crisp cracker such as a pita chip or a flat bread.

Camembert cheese: Is soft ripened, creamy and strongly flavored. It is perfectly paired with a crusty baguette and crunchy apples.

Cheddar cheese: Is a hard cheese with a tangy and sharp flavor. It is delicious eaten on its own cubed or sliced onto a cracker. It goes well with almonds and olives.

Hard Parmigiano: Is a rich, full cheese with a hard, granular texture. When young, it is fruity and mild. It can age up to 5 years. Serve on bread, salads or any pasta dish.

Mozzarella: Has a semi firm texture, is low in moisture, and is mild in taste. The braided mozzarella comes in a spicy version. Serve as an appetizer on toasted bread with tomatoes and herbs.

Mozzarella balls: Is fresh mozzarella contained in a brine or olive oil with low saltiness and natural sweetness. The cheese should appear moister than regular mozzarella. Serve with tomatoes and top with a dash of olive oil and balsamic vinegar.

cook's note

Serve fresh soft cheeses, such as Brie, whole and provide a knife to cut and spread it onto crackers or bread. Semi-soft cheeses should be served in cut pieces. Semi-hard cheeses and soft ripened cheeses should be cut into wedges. Hard cheeses should be pre-cut into small pieces. Blue cheeses should be served in crumbles which you can make with your cheese knife.

prep time
35 minutes

cook time
30 minutes

serves
6

plan ahead

Figs and syrup can be made a day ahead. Store in separate containers, cover and refrigerate. Rewarm syrup before using; it will harden when chilled.

Walnut streusel can be made up to 2 days ahead. Store in an airtight container at room temperature.

simplify

Use candied pecans in place of walnuts. Use high-quality fig jam, warmed slightly, in place of fresh figs.

cheese and fig tartlets with walnut streusel and pomegranate syrup

When the sharp creaminess of blue cheese is balanced by the tart sweetness of pomegranate, flavors mingle in perfect harmony....a symphony of tastes! Try this unique starter or hors d'oeuvre for your next special event.

- ½ cup sugar
- 1 tablespoon water
- Pinch of salt
- 9 fresh figs (preferably Black Mission), stemmed, cut in half lengthwise
- ¼ cup (½ stick) unsalted butter
- 1 sheet frozen puff pastry (½ of 17.3-ounce package), thawed

- Walnut Streusel *(recipe below)*
- 2-3 ounces crumbly firm cheese, preferably blue cheese, coarsely crumbled, room temperature (use less cheese if using blue cheese)
- ½ cup pomegranate molasses

garnish
- Honeycomb, cut into pieces or honey

Filling: In a large, heavy large skillet over medium heat, stir sugar, water and salt until combined. Cook until sugar begins to turn golden, about 4 minutes, stirring occasionally (mixture may be granular). Place figs, cut side down, in sugar mixture, and cook until figs begin to release juice, about 3 minutes. Add butter and swirl the skillet to melt. Remove from heat. Add molasses and let stand for 5 minutes. Using a slotted spoon, transfer figs to a plate and cool. Return syrup to a boil, whisking until smooth. Remove from heat and cool completely.

Bake: Preheat oven to 350°. Line a baking sheet with parchment paper. Roll out puff pastry on a lightly floured surface to a 12x8-inch rectangle. Using a 3½-inch round cutter, cut out 6 rounds; arrange on prepared sheet. Divide walnut streusel evenly among pastry rounds. Top each with 3 fig halves, cut side up. Bake tartlets until pastry is puffed and golden, about 30 minutes. Arrange cheese atop warm tartlets. Brush or drizzle with warm pomegranate molasses; then top with honeycomb cube or drizzle with honey.

walnut streusel

- 2 tablespoons honey
- 2 tablespoons sugar
- 1 tablespoon butter
- 1 tablespoon flour

- ⅛ teaspoon ground cinnamon
- ⅛ teaspoon salt
- 6 tablespoons chopped walnuts, toasted

In a medium skillet over medium-high heat, stir together honey, sugar, butter, flour, cinnamon and salt until sugar melts. Cook until mixture boils and is a deep golden brown, about 3 minutes. Mix in walnuts and pour onto a sheet of foil; cool completely. Chop into small pieces.

broccoli cheese and herb bread ring

An outstanding addition to any meal, this savory bread stays moist and tender as Parmesan cheese melts bakes into it.

prep time
25 minutes plus
1 hour dough
rising time

cook time
50-60 minutes

serves
8

- 2½ cups flour
- 1 egg yolk
- 8 tablespoons (1 stick) butter, melted, divided
- Salt, to taste
- 1 teaspoon active dry yeast
- ¾ cup milk, warmed
- 2 tablespoons extra- virgin olive oil
- 1 head broccoli, cut into small pieces
- 1 teaspoon finely chopped fresh oregano
- 1 tablespoon finely chopped fresh parsley
- 1 tablespoon finely chopped fresh chives
- ½ cup pine nuts
- 6 ounces parmesan cheese, cubed

Dough: In the bowl of a standing electric mixer, combine flour, egg yolk, 2 tablespoons butter and salt. In a separate small bowl, dissolve yeast in milk. Add to flour mixture. Mix until a homogenous and elastic dough forms. Cover and set aside to rise until doubled in volume, about 30 minutes.

Cook: In a large skillet, heat oil over medium heat. Add broccoli and season with salt. Add oregano, parsley, chives and pine nuts, and sauté for about 7 minutes. Set aside.

Fill: Preheat oven to 350°. On a lightly floured surface, roll out dough to a rounded long rectangle, 1-inch thick. Brush with 6 tablespoons of butter and distribute broccoli mixture and cubed parmesan along the center. Roll over to form a cylinder, and pinch to close. Fit the cylinder into a buttered bundt pan to make a ring. Set aside to rise until it fills the mold, about 30 minutes.

Bake: Bake for 50-60 minutes, or until golden brown. Unmold and serve warm.

recipes featured on pages 236-237   235

cheddar cheese cracker rounds

prep time
15 minutes

cook time
22 minutes

yields
50 cracker
rounds

Cheddar cheese is known for it's firm texture, deep color and sharpness. In these cracker rounds, cheddar lends its own distinctive flavor and binds them, making these crackers stand apart from the rest.

- 2 cups flour
- 16 ounces extra sharp cheddar cheese, **coarsely grated**
- ¾ cup (1½ sticks) chilled unsalted butter, **diced**
- 1 teaspoon salt
- 2 tablespoons chilled heavy cream
- Assorted seasoning
  (sesame seeds, pecan halves, ground nutmeg, celery seed, poppy seeds)

Prep: Preheat oven to 350°. Line 2 baking sheets with parchment paper. In the bowl of a food processor, fitted with an "S" blade, combine flour, cheese, butter and salt. Blend until cheese is finely chopped. Add cream and blend until moist clumps form.

Bake: Pour seasonings into separate shallow plates. Roll dough into balls, using 1 level tablespoon dough for each. Roll each ball in a garnish, pressing lightly so it will adhere. Alternately, place a pecan half in the center of a ball. Place on prepared cooking sheets, spacing them 1 inch apart. Bake until cooked through and golden brown on bottom, about 22 minutes, rotating sheets halfway through baking.

onion-olive focaccia

A delicious artisanal bread that lends itself to any type of meal. Think long hot summer days -- served with a cheese spread. Or lightly toasted and served with soup on a cold, winter's day.

- 2¾ to 3¼ cups all-purpose flour, **divided**
- 1 (¼-ounce) package active dry yeast
- ½ teaspoon salt
- 1 cup warm water
- 4 tablespoons olive oil, **divided**

- 3 medium sweet onions, **halved and sliced**
- 2 cloves garlic, **minced**
- 2 teaspooons fresh rosemary, **chopped or** ¾ teaspoon dried rosemary, **crushed**
- ½ cup sliced, **pitted green olives**

prep time
30 minutes
plus 30 minutes
rising time

cook time
30 minutes

serves
6-8

plan ahead

This bread freezes well. Double wrap tightly in foil and freeze until needed.

Dough: In the bowl of a standing electric mixer, combine 1¼ cups flour, yeast and salt. Add water and 2 tablespoons oil. Beat on low speed for 30 seconds, scraping bowl constantly. Raise mixer to high speed and continue to beat for 3 minutes. Using a wooden spoon, mix in 1 cup flour. If still wet, gradually add more. Turn out onto a lightly floured surface. Knead for 6-8 minutes, adding flour as needed, to make a moderately stiff dough that is smooth and elastic. Cover and let rest for 10 minutes.

Onion-olive topping: In a medium skillet, heat remaining 2 tablespoons oil over medium heat. Add onions, garlic and rosemary, and cook over low heat for 15 minutes or until very tender, stirring occasionally. Remove from heat. Stir in olives and set aside.

Prepare focaccia: Turn dough out on lightly floured surface. Divide in half. Roll each portion into a 10-inch circle. Transfer to a lightly greased baking sheet. With fingertips, press slight indentations all over dough rounds. Top evenly with onion-olive topping. Cover and let rise in a warm place until nearly doubled in size, about 30-40 minutes.

Bake: Preheat oven to 375°. Bake foccacia for 25-30 minutes or until golden. Cut into wedges. Serve warm or at room temperature.

239

zucchini crowned quiche

With its regal crown, grace your Shavuos table with a quiche fit for a king! Rich and creamy, a wonderful dairy entree or side dish.

prep time
30 minutes

cook time
45 minutes

serves
8

- 5 tablespoons extra virgin olive oil, divided
- 3 scallions, white and light-green parts only, finely chopped
- Salt and pepper to taste
- 8 slices Italian bread, cubed and lightly toasted
- 2 medium zucchini, thinly sliced
- 1 teaspoon fresh thyme, chopped
- 4 eggs
- 3½ ounces ricotta cheese
- ⅓ cup heavy cream
- 1 teaspoon nutmeg
- Pinch of salt
- Flour, for dusting
- 1 pound frozen puff pastry, thawed
- 4 ounces baby gouda cheese, cubed
- 4 ounces sharp cheddar cheese, cubed
- ½ cup parmesan cheese, freshly grated

Vegetable and cheese filling: In a large skillet, heat 3 tablespoons oil over medium heat. Add scallions and sauté until slightly soft, about 7 minutes. Season with salt and pepper and add bread cubes. Saute for about 10 minutes and set aside. In a separate skillet, heat remaining 2 tablespoons oil over medium heat. Add zucchini and thyme, season with salt and pepper and saute for 7 minutes. Set aside. In a large bowl, combine eggs, ricotta cheese, heavy cream, nutmeg and salt. Add scallions and bread cubes, and mix well.

Prepare dough: Preheat oven to 350°. On a lightly floured surface, roll out puff pastry to a 1/10-inch thickness. Transfer to a 9-inch round springform pan, and press with your fingers to line the pan with the dough. Fold overhanging dough back over itself and press firmly, creating a thicker layer on the sides. Trim any excess dough. Spread ricotta mixture and top with cubed cheese. Arrange zucchini in a layer over mixture, and sprinkle with parmesan. Bake for 30 minutes, remove pan from the oven. Carefully remove the ring from around the springform, without breaking the crust. Place pan back in the oven and continue to bake for another 10-15 or until golden brown.

prep time
5 minutes

cook time
5-7 minutes

yields
2 cups

plan ahead
Can be prepared
up two days
ahead and stored,
covered, in the
refrigerator.

goat cheese spread
with apricot mango chutney

Goat cheese is a mellow-flavored soft cheese that pairs beautifully with tangy fruits. Gently mixed together with an apricot mango chutney is the perfect balance of tangy, salty and sweet. Use as a spread on brioche or no-knead bread for a simple slice of goodness.
Spread featured here on slices of brioche, recipe on page 236.

- 1 (8-ounce) package cream cheese, softened
- 3½ ounces feta cheese, crumbled
- 3½ ounces goat cheese, crumbled
- Apricot Mango Chutney *(recipe below)*

Prep: Place cream cheese in a bowl and beat until creamy. Add feta and goat cheeses and beat until well blended. Add chutney and whip on low speed in a blender until well blended. Cover and chill for one hour.

apricot mango chutney

- 1 tablespoon honey
- 3 tablespoons apricot preserves
- 1 tablespopon balsamic vinegar
- 2 tablespoons dried minced onions
- 1 tablespoon chopped red onion
- 1 tablespoon chopped fresh thyme
- 1 tablespoon chopped fresh cilantro
- ½ small (¼ cup) unripe mango, chopped

In a small saucepan over medium heat combine honey, preserves, vinegar, onions, thyme and cilantro until thickened. Let cool to room temperature and stir in mango.

mom's pastries' quesadilla wraps

CONTRIBUTED BY MOM'S PASTRIES OF CEDARHURST, NEW YORK

Quick, tasty and kid-friendly. Who could ask for anything more?

prep time
5 minutes

cook time
15 minutes

serves
2

- 2 (12-inch) round wraps, any flavor
- 1 red bell pepper, halved and seeded
- 1 teaspoon olive oil
- Kosher salt, to taste
- 4 ounces shredded mozzarella cheese
- 1 beef tomato, sliced into rounds
- 1 medium red onion, sliced into thin rounds
- ½ cup sliced cremini mushrooms
- Chopped Tomato Salsa *(recipe below)*

simplify
Use purchased roasted red pepper strips.

cook's note
Chopped tomato salsa would be delicious as bruschetta on bread.

Roast Peppers: Place oven rack about 3-4 inches from the top of the oven. Preheat oven to 500°. Place pepper halves on a foil-lined baking sheet, cut side up. Brush the inside of peppers with oil and sprinkle with salt. Turn over and roast until skin is charred and blistering, about 15 minutes. Remove from oven, cover with foil and cool for at least 10 minutes. Remove foil and carefully peel away the pepper skins from the flesh. Discard skins and cut each pepper half into 2 pieces.

Wrap: Lay wraps on a work surface. Layer each wrap with 2 roasted red pepper slices, 2 ounces cheese, 2-3 tomato slices and 2-3 onion slices. Fold in edges of each wrap and roll up, jellyroll style. Place wraps in a panini or sandwich maker until marks appear, about 5-7 minutes. Cut each in half and serve with Chopped Tomato Salsa.

chopped tomato salsa

- 1 shallot, diced
- 4 plum tomatoes, diced
- 1 clove garlic, crushed
- Salt and pepper, to taste
- 1 teaspoon oil

- 1 teaspoon purchased pesto sauce
- 1 tablespoon chopped fresh cilantro
- 1 tablespoon chopped fresh parsley

optional
- ¼ cup feta cheese, crumbled

In a medium bowl, combine all ingredients and mix well.

prep time
30 minutes

cook time
50 minutes plus
pasta cooking
time

serves
8-10

simplify

*Use purchased
marinara sauce in
place of red pepper
sauce. While you
cannot compare
the taste, the color
has the same effect
when serving.*

spinach and cheese pinwheels
with roasted red pepper sauce

*The bright beautiful colors of red pepper and spinach make these curly pinwheel lasagnas
a visual delight.*

- 2 tablespoons butter, plus extra for baking dish
- 1 (16-ounce) package frozen chopped spinach, thawed
- 1 cup ricotta cheese
- 8 ounces fresh goat cheese, crumbled
- ⅛ teaspoon ground nutmeg
- Salt and pepper, to taste
- 2 eggs, lightly beaten
- 1 (16 ounce) box curly edged lasagna noodles
- ¼ cup (½ stick) butter, melted
- ¼ cup heavy cream
- Roasted Red Pepper Sauce *(recipe to the right)*

Spinach filling: In a medium skillet, heat butter over medium heat. Add spinach and cook,
stirring constantly, until all the moisture has evaporated, 2-3 minutes. Remove from heat and
allow to cool slightly. Stir in ricotta cheese, goat cheese, nutmeg, salt and pepper. Add eggs and
mix well.

Pasta Rolls: Cook pasta according to package directions. Stir gently from time to time to keep
from sticking. Lift out noodles with a slotted spatula and place in a bowl of cold water. Drain and
spread noodles out on a clean dish towel to drain thoroughly. Butter a baking dish and preheat
the oven to 375°. Using a metal spatula or spoon, spread 3-4 tablespoons spinach filling on each
noodle, leaving a ¼-inch border. Roll noodles into neat cylinders and arrange in the buttered
baking dish.

Cream sauce: Mix melted butter with heavy cream and pour over rolls. Cover the dish tightly
with buttered foil and bake until a skewer inserted in the center of a roll is hot to the touch when
withdrawn, about 30 minutes.

Serve: Heat red pepper sauce and spoon onto a serving platter. Cut each roll in half crosswise
and stand on the sauce. Garnish with basil sprigs. Serve remaining sauce separately. Can also be
served individually; stand 2 pinwheels in a puddle of sauce on each individual plate.

roasted red pepper sauce

- 2 tablespoons olive oil
- 3 cloves garlic, chopped
- 4 scallions, chopped
- 4 red bell peppers, roasted, peeled and chopped
- 2 tomatoes, peeled, seeded and chopped
- 6 basil leaves, sliced into small pieces, plus more for garnish
- Salt and pepper, to taste

In a medium skillet, heat olive oil over medium heat. Add garlic, scallions, peppers, tomatoes and basil. Cook until thickened, about 15-20 minutes, stirring occasionally. Puree in a food processor fitted with an "S" blade until almost smooth. Season with salt and pepper.

spaghetti
with creamy braised garlic and leeks

Leeks are often the unsung hero of the onion family. Never underestimate their sweet, subtle onion flavor which can add tremendous depth to a dish. Here they are featured as the star of the show.

prep time
20 minutes

cook time
45 minutes

serves
6

- 12 ounces spaghetti
- 2 tablespoons butter
- 4 leeks, halved and sliced
- 6 cloves garlic, halved
- ½ teaspoon salt, plus more to taste
- ¼ teaspoon pepper, plus more to taste
- ¼ cup dry white wine
- 1 cup vegetable broth
- ½ cup heavy cream
- ¼ cup parmesan cheese, finely grated

garnish
- Fresh parsley, chopped

cook's note

Leeks can be full of grit and sand. To clean them, cut in half lengthwise and, using running water, wash very well between each piece.

Pasta: Cook pasta according to package directions, reserving ½ cup cooking water. Set aside.

Sauce: In a medium skillet, melt butter over medium-low heat. Add leeks, garlic, salt and pepper. Cook until leeks brown, stirring often, about 5 minutes. Add wine and simmer, covered, until reduced to half, about 8 minutes. Add broth and simmer for an additional 30 minutes, until leeks and garlic are very soft. Remove from the flame. Add cream and stir until sauce thickens.

Serve: Place spaghetti in a serving dish with reserved pasta water. Pour leeks over pasta and toss to combine. Add parmesan cheese and season to taste with salt and pepper. Garnish with parsley and serve.

plan ahead

Pesto sauce freezes well and can be frozen in ice cube trays to create individual serving portions.

farfalle
with red wine vinegar pesto sauce

Pesto sauce is Italian in origin, and traditionally made with garlic, basil and pine nuts. Our addition of red wine vinegar lends the sauce a splash of acidity to boost its flavor.

- 1 (1 pound) box farfalle (bow-tie shaped pasta)
- ½ cup fresh basil
- 4 teaspoons red wine vinegar
- 1 clove garlic

- 1 teaspoon salt
- Freshly ground black pepper, to taste
- 1 cup olive oil

garnish
- Freshly shaved parmesan curls

Pasta: Cook pasta according to package directions. Set aside.

Pesto: In a food processor fitted with and "S" blade, puree basil, vinegar, garlic, salt and pepper. Add oil in a slow stream while the food processor is running. Pour pesto over warm pasta, tossing gently. Garnish with parmesan curls and serve.

basil spinach fettuccine with broiled mozzarella tomatoes

Broiling garden fresh tomatoes brings out their natural sweetness and earthy essence. Top that with sizzling melted cheese and this dish is a winner!

prep time
10 minutes

cook time
10 minutes
plus pasta
cooking time

serves
6

- 1 (1pound) box spinach fettuccine
- 3 large beefsteak tomatoes, each cut into 4 slices
- 8 ounces fresh mozzarella, grated
- 3 tablespoons olive oil
- 1 ounce (¼ cup) fresh parmesan cheese, grated, plus more, shaved for garnish
- 2 cloves garlic, chopped

- ⅓ teaspoon crushed red pepper flakes
- ¾ teaspoon kosher salt, divided
- ½ teaspoon black pepper, divided

garnish
- ¾ cup chopped fresh basil leaves
- 2 teaspoons chopped fresh thyme

Fettuccine: Cook pasta according to package directions, drain and return to the pot.

Broil tomatoes: Preheat broiler to medium. Arrange tomato slices on a baking sheet coated with nonstick cooking spray. Season with ¼ teaspoon each of salt and pepper. Sprinkle mozzarella and parmesan cheeses evenly over tomatoes. Broil until cheese is bubbly, about 3-5 minutes.

Sauce: In a small saucepan, over medium heat, warm oil with garlic and red pepper flakes until fragrant, about 1-2 minutes. Add garlic oil, ¼ teaspoon salt and ¼ teaspoon pepper to pasta, tossing to combine.

Serve: Top plated pasta with tomatoes. Garnish with basil and shaved parmesan.

lasagna wonton stacks
with tomato basil sauce

Lasagna is a popular dish with children and adults alike. Try this version for a clean individual presentation and shorter prep time.

prep time
25 minutes
cook time
30 minutes
serves
8

simplify

Used purchased marinara sauce for homemade sauce.

- 1 clove garlic, minced
- 1 tablespoon unsalted butter
- 1 (14.5-ounce) can crushed tomatoes
- 4 tablespoons fresh basil, finely chopped, divided
- 1 tablespoon fresh orange juice, or to taste
- Salt and pepper, to taste
- ¾ cup whole-milk ricotta cheese
- ¼ cup parmesan cheese, freshly grated
- 1 egg
- 2 teaspoons fresh oregano, finely chopped
- 12 eggroll skins, (from a package of refrigerated wonton skins, or eggroll wrappers, such as NaSoya brand)
- 6 ounces shredded mozzarella cheese

garnish
- Fresh basil leaves

Tomato sauce: Preheat oven to 400°. In a large, heavy saucepan over medium heat, cook garlic in butter, stirring for 1 minute. Add tomatoes with liquid and 2 tablespoons basil. Simmer uncovered over medium heat, for 20 minutes, stirring occasionally. Stir in orange juice, salt and pepper.

Prep: In a medium bowl, mix ricotta cheese, parmesan cheese, egg, remaining basil, oregano, salt and pepper. In a 6-quart pot, boil salted water. Separate eggroll skins and add to boiling water. Using a slotted spoon, immediately transfer to a shallow dish filled with cold water.

Layer lasagna: Spread ½ cup tomato sauce evenly on bottom of a buttered 13x9x2-inch glass baking dish. Arrange 4 eggroll skins, drained briefly on a kitchen towel, in one layer on top of sauce. Divide half of ricotta mixture evenly among the squares in the pan and top with 4 more skins, drained briefly. Spoon remaining ricotta mixture evenly on these skins and top with remaining 4 skins, drained. Spoon several tablespoons sauce over each stack and top with shredded mozzarella. Bake, uncovered, in middle of oven until bubbling and heated through, about 10 minutes.

Garnish with a fresh basil leaf on each stack and serve.

prep time
15 minutes

cook time
1 hour
plus pasta
cooking time

serves
8

plan ahead
The timballo may
be prepared up
to 2 days ahead.
Store covered in
the refrigerator,
unmolded. To
serve, reheat in
the oven for 15-20
minutes at 300°.
Unmold as per the
recipe directions.

simplify
In a pinch, you
can get the look
of the timballo,
minus some of the
work (and flavor).
Instead of the
creamed spinach,
substitute spinach
mixed with ½ cup
heavy cream and
1 teaspoon salt.
Use plain marinara
sauce in place of
the sauce recipe.

creamed spinach and red wine timballo

A timballo is a dome-shaped Italian casserole usually made with pasta, rice or potatoes. In this timballo, a layer of creamed spinach adds extra creaminess and color to the dish.

special equipment
- 2-quart soufflé dish or dome shaped glass mixing bowl
- Parchment paper

sauce
- 1½ cups marinara sauce
- 1 stalk celery, finely chopped
- 1 tablespoon tomato paste
- ½ cup dry red wine
- Pinch of sugar

- 12 ounces ziti
- 2 tablespoons unsalted butter
- 2 garlic cloves, minced
- 1 tablespoon all-purpose flour
- 1 (10-ounce) box frozen chopped spinach, thawed and drained
- 1 cup whole milk
- ¼ teaspoon salt
- ⅛ teaspoon white pepper
- ⅛ teaspoon fresh nutmeg, finely grated
- 1 ounce (½ cup) parmesan cheese, freshly grated, divided
- 4 ounces (scant 1 cup) fresh mozzarella, cut into ½-inch cubes

Prepare sauce: Heat marinara sauce in a large heavy skillet over medium heat until hot. Add celery, tomato paste, wine and sugar. Cook, stirring constantly, until most of liquid is evaporated, about 5 minutes. Set aside and let cool.

Pasta: Prepare pasta according to package directions. Drain, but do not rinse. Set aside.

Creamed spinach: Heat butter in a 1½-2-quart heavy saucepan over medium heat until foam subsides. Add garlic and stir for 1 minute. Add flour and cook for 1 minute. Add milk in a slow stream, whisking. Bring to a boil, whisking. Reduce heat and simmer, whisking occasionally, until sauce is slightly thickened, about 5 minutes. Stir in spinach, salt, pepper, nutmeg and 2 tablespoons parmesan cheese. Remove the pan from heat.

Assembly: Place oven rack in lower third of oven and preheat oven to 375°. Grease a soufflé dish or domed glass mixing bowl, and line bottom with greased foil. Cover bottom of the dish or bowl with a single layer of pasta. Sprinkle ½ cup cubed mozzarella and 3 tablespoons parmesan over pasta. Spoon half of sauce in an even layer over cheese. Arrange one third of remaining pasta over sauce and top with all of creamed spinach. Add another layer of pasta (about half of remainder). Sprinkle with remainder of cheeses. Spoon remaining sauce over cheese. Top with remaining pasta. (You may have some pasta remaining.) Spray a piece of foil with cooking spray and cover pasta.

Bake: Place the dish into a 9x13-inch baking dish. Fill the 9x13 dish with water halfway up the sides of the soufflé dish. Bake until bubbling and a metal skewer or thin knife inserted in center of timballo comes out hot to the touch, about 1 hour. Remove soufflé dish or bowl from water bath and let stand, covered, for 15 minutes. Remove foil and run a knife around edge of timballo to loosen. Place a platter on the soufflé dish and invert the dish onto the platter. Remove the soufflé dish or bowl and remaining foil.

fusilli pasta
with olive garlic tapenade

A tapenade is a smooth paste made from olives with a variety of different seasonings. In this version, green olives get a boost of flavor from fresh herbs and garlic.

prep time
15 minutes
cook time
15 minutes
serves
8

- 1 (1 pound) box fusilli pasta
- 1 tablespoon extra-virgin olive oil
- 2 pints cherry tomatoes, halved
- 2 tablespoons chopped fresh thyme
- 2 tablespoons chopped fresh oregano
- Salt and pepper, to taste
- Olive Garlic Tapenade *(recipe below)*

Pasta: Cook pasta according to package directions. Transfer to a large bowl. Drizzle oil over pasta; toss to coat. Cool, stirring occasionally. Add tomatoes, thyme, oregano and tapenade to pasta; toss to coat. Season with salt and pepper.

plan ahead
Tapenade can be made up to 3 days ahead. Store covered in refrigerator.

simplify
Use purchased olive tapenade instead of making your own.

olive garlic tapenade

- 1 clove garlic, peeled
- 2 cups sliced green olives, divided
- 3 tablespoons capers, drained
- 1 tablespoon red wine vinegar
- 1 tablespoon Dijon mustard
- ¼ teaspoon crushed red pepper flakes
- ½ cup extra-virgin olive oil

Add garlic through the feed tube of a food processor fitted with an "S" blade while the machine is running, and process until finely chopped; turn off machine. Add 1 cup olives, capers, vinegar, mustard and red pepper flakes. Using the pulse feature, process until a coarse paste forms. With machine running, add oil in a slow stream, forming a coarse pureé. Transfer to a bowl and stir in remaining olives. Season with salt and pepper.

cook's note

*Gnocchi are best
served fresh.*

gnocchi with vegetable ragout

*Gnocchi are small Italian potato dumplings, similar to pasta dumplings. They are delicious when
served with tomato sauce, pesto or a vegetable ragout such as this.*

- 4 tablespoons extra-virgin olive oil, divided
- 1 medium onion (½ cup), diced
- 2 small carrots, peeled and diced
- 1 stalk celery, diced
- 8 ounces mixed wild mushrooms (e.g., cremini, oyster, baby bella), stems removed and diced
- Kosher salt and freshly ground black pepper, to taste
- 1 (16-ounce) can mushrooms, drained
- 2 tablespoons tomato paste
- 1 cup dry red wine
- 1 (32-ounce) can best quality whole tomatoes, diced, liquid reserved
- 1 cup water
- 2 bay leaves
- ½ teaspoon ground coriander
- ½ teaspoon ground fennel seeds
- Pinch of crushed red pepper flakes
- 1 tablespoon fresh thyme, chopped
- ½ teaspoon salt
- 2 (1-pound) packages prepared gnocchi

  garnish
- Sour cream
- Parmesan cheese, freshly shaved or grated

Prepare sauce: In a large pot, heat 2 tablespoons oil over medium-high heat. Add onion, carrots
and celery and cook until soft, about 5 minutes. Add fresh mushrooms and cook until softened,
5 to 7 minutes. Season with salt and pepper. Add canned mushrooms and tomato paste, stirring
with a wooden spoon, about 2 minutes. Add wine; cook, scraping up any browned bits, about
2 more minutes. Add tomatoes, water, bay leaves, coriander, fennel seeds, red pepper flakes,
thyme and salt. Simmer uncovered over medium heat, about 30 minutes (dilute with water if
needed). Season again with salt and pepper.

Gnocchi: Cook gnocchi according to package directions. Transfer with a slotted spoon to a
serving dish. Top with hot ragout sauce. Serve topped with dollop of sour cream and parmesan.

desserts

summer fruit medley
with cinnamon-ginger reduction

Spice up a simple fruit salad with this ginger-infused dressing – an invigorating twist that your family will love!

prep time
20 minutes

cook time
15 minutes

serves
6

- 1 tablespoon lime zest (from 4 limes)
- 1 (2-inch) piece fresh ginger, **peeled**
- 1 tablespoon fresh lemon juice (from 1 small lemon)
- 1 teaspoon cinnamon
- ½ teaspoon cardamom
- 1 cup fresh lime juice (from about 8 limes)
- ¼ cup sugar
- Pinch of salt
- ½ small ripe honeydew melon, **seeds and rind removed, cut into 1-inch pieces** (about 2 cups)
- 1 ripe mango, **peeled and cut into ½-inch pieces**
- 1 pint blueberries
- 3 tablespoons chopped crystallized ginger

Reduce: Combine lime zest, ginger, lemon juice, cinnamon and cardamom in a small bowl; set aside. Combine lime juice, sugar and salt in a small, heavy, nonreactive saucepan over high heat. Simmer until syrupy and honey-colored, about 15 minutes–mixture should be reduced to ¼ cup. Remove pan from heat and add ginger mixture. Steep for 2 minutes and strain.

Assemble: Combine fruit in a medium bowl and pour warm strained dressing over fruit; toss to coat. Sprinkle chopped crystallized ginger over fruit. Serve immediately at room temperature or cover and refrigerate up to 4 hours. Serve chilled.

Serving Option: For an elegant brunch option, serve individual portions spooned over Greek yogurt in parfait glasses.

prep time
35 minutes

cook time
35 minutes plus
chilling time

yields
42 bars

plan ahead
Bars may be made
up to 3 days ahead
and refrigerated,
covered.

cook's note
For perfectly
clean slices, dip
knife in hot water,
cleaning the blade
in between cutting
pieces.

double chocolate swirl bars

You can never go wrong with a decadent chocolate mousse bar. Using good quality chocolate makes all the difference.

cookie crust
- 1 cup flour
- ⅔ cup cocoa powder
- ½ cup (1 stick) butter or margarine, softened
- 1 cup confectioner's sugar
- 1 egg yolk
- ½ teaspoon vanilla extract

mousse
- 1½ cups heavy whipping cream or frozen non-dairy dessert whip topping, **defrosted**
- ¼ cup sugar
- 1 teaspoon vanilla extract
- 2 cups semisweet baking chocolate (about 12 ounces), **chopped**
- 4 large eggs

chocolate swirl topping
- 8 ounces white chocolate, **broken into pieces**
- 2 tablespoons solid vegetable shortening
- 2 tablespoons semisweet baking chocolate (½ ounce), **finely chopped**

Prep: Preheat oven to 350°. Line a 9x13x2-inch baking pan with foil, letting foil extend about 2 inches above the ends of the pan. Grease foil with cooking spray.

Crust: Whisk flour and cocoa in a small bowl to blend; set aside. Combine butter or margarine, confectioner's sugar, egg yolk and vanilla in a large bowl. Using an electric mixer, beat on medium speed for 1-2 minutes until fluffy. Scrape down the sides of the bowl and add flour mixture. Beat on low speed for 1-2 minutes or until moist clumps form. Scatter the mixture over the bottom of the prepared pan. Press into an even layer. Bake for about 10 minutes or until crust looks puffy and dry. Transfer the pan to a wire rack to cool. Meanwhile, prepare mousse.

Mousse: Combine whipping cream or whip topping, sugar and vanilla in a microwave-safe bowl to blend. Microwave on high for 2-3 minutes until mixture barely starts to simmer. Add chocolate and let sit for 1-2 minutes. Whisk until chocolate melts and mixture is smooth. Cool for 6-8 minutes. Whisk in eggs, 1 at a time, until blended. Pour mixture over hot crust. Bake for 30-32 minutes, until edges rise slightly higher than center and mousse may look cracked.

Chocolate Swirl: Melt white chocolate and shortening in a small saucepan over low heat. Stir until smooth. Pour white chocolate over hot mousse and spread evenly. Place semisweet chocolate in a small bowl and microwave in 15-second increments, stirring in between each 15 seconds until chocolate is melted and smooth. Transfer to a zip top bag; snip tip off one corner and pipe thick chocolate stripes over white chocolate. Draw a toothpick through chocolate for marbled effect. Refrigerate, uncovered, for 2 hours until glaze hardens.

Serve: Holding foil ends, lift out whole sheet of bars and transfer to a cutting board. Using a sharp knife, gently cut crosswise into 6 long strips. Cut each strip into 7 triangles. Refrigerate, covered, until serving time.

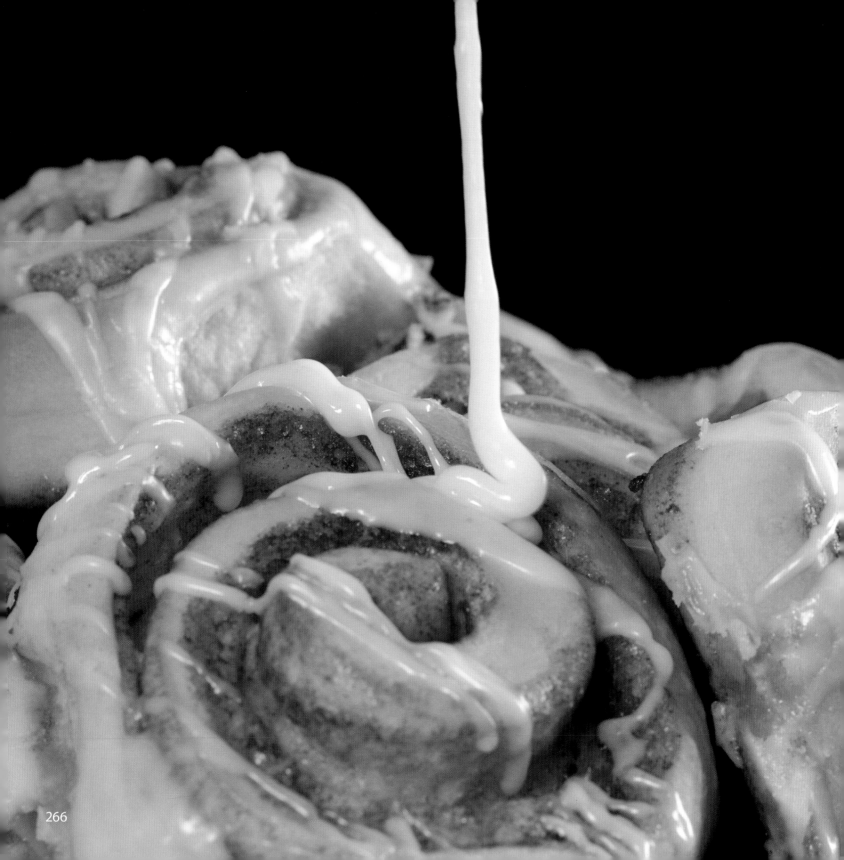

ooey gooey cinnamon buns

These cinnamon buns are not for the faint of heart. Get your coffee at the ready for a delectable morning treat or enjoy this perfect choice for breaking a fast.

prep time
30 minutes
plus 2-2½ hours
rising time

cook time
30-35 minutes

yields
24 buns

plan ahead
Dough can rise overnight in the refrigerator.

dough
- 2 cups warm water
- 1 teaspoon sugar
- 2 ounces fresh yeast or 3-section package dry yeast
- 1 cup sugar
- 1 cup (2 sticks) butter or margarine, melted
- 4 eggs
- ¼ cup vanilla sugar
- 1 teaspoon salt
- 8 cups flour (more, as needed)

filling
- 4 cups dark brown sugar
- 8 teaspoons cinnamon
- 1 pound (4 sticks) butter or margarine, melted

glaze
- ½ cup confectioner's sugar
- 8 teaspoons water

Proof: In a small glass bowl or measuring cup, combine warm water, 1 teaspoon sugar and yeast. Dissolve and let sit for 10 minutes, until bubbles or foam form.

Mix: In a separate large bowl, combine 1 cup sugar, butter or margarine, eggs, vanilla sugar and salt. Mix to blend. Add in yeast mixture and then flour, adding a little at a time until dough comes away from sides of the bowl. Knead for 1-2 minutes, until dough is a cohesive mass. Cover with a dish towel and let dough rise for 1½-2 hours–dough should be doubled in bulk.

Fill: Combine brown sugar and cinnamon in a medium bowl; set aside. Punch down dough and divide into 2 parts. Roll out each part into a large rectangle (about 11x17-inches) on a floured work surface. Spread an even layer of melted butter or margarine over entire dough's surface. Sprinkle an even layer of brown sugar mixture on top. Carefully roll up each dough lengthwise (jellyroll style). Using a sharp knife, slice roll into 1½-inch-thick slices. Lay each slice flat, tucking and wrapping the ends to shape individual buns. Place buns in an even layer in 2 greased 9x13-inch pans or press buns together in 2 greased 9-inch round pans to form a cinnamon bun breakaway cake. Let rise for 30 minutes.

Bake: Preheat oven to 350°. Bake 9x13-inch pans about 45 minutes, until tops are lightly browned, checking after 40 minutes; bake 9-inch round pans for 30-35 minutes, until tops are lightly browned, checking after 30 minutes.

Glaze: Combine sugar and water in a small bowl to form glaze. Brush heavily with glaze immediately after baking. Apply a second coat when slightly cooled.

prep time	
10 minutes	
cook time	
20-25 minutes	
yields	
24 cupcakes	

white chocolate peach cupcakes
with lemon buttercream frosting

These cupcakes are a bite of summer. And with the innovative use of a cake mix, you will be in and out of the kitchen in time to enjoy the day.

plan ahead

Cupcakes may be frozen, unfrosted, for up to a month. Thaw overnight in the refrigerator before serving. Cupcakes may be prepared and frosted up to a week in advance and stored in the refrigerator.

simplify

Use purchased white frosting and mix in lemon juice and lemon zest.

cook's note

Frosting makes 3½ cups, enough to frost a 2 or 3 layer cake or 30 cupcakes.

cake

- 6 ounces white chocolate, **finely chopped**
- 6 tablespoons (¾ stick) margarine, **cut into pieces**
- 1 package (18.25 ounces) plain white or golden yellow cake mix
- 1 cup soy milk
- 3 large eggs
- 1 teaspoon pure vanilla extract
- 1 cup fresh peaches, **peeled and chopped (2 large peaches)**
- ½ cup Lemon Buttercream Frosting

garnish

- 2 peaches, **sliced into thin slivers**
- ½ cup peach jam

lemon buttercream frosting

- 8 tablespoons (1 stick) margarine, **at room temperature**
- 4 cups confectioner's sugar, **sifted**
- 2-3 tablespoons soy milk
- 1 tablespoon fresh lemon juice
- 1 tablespoon lemon zest, **grated**

Prep Cake: Place oven rack in the center of oven and preheat to 350. Line 24 muffin cups with paper liners. Place white chocolate and margarine in a small saucepan over low heat. Cook, stirring, until both have melted, about 3-4 minutes. Let cool slightly.

Mix: Place cake mix, soy milk, eggs, vanilla and white chocolate mixture in a large mixing bowl. Blend with mixer on low speed for 1 minute. Stop the machine and scrape down the sides of the bowl with a rubber spatula. Increase the mixer speed to medium and blend for 2 more minutes, scraping down the sides again if needed. Batter should be well combined. Fold in peaches. Spoon batter into the lined muffin cups, filling each ⅔ of the way full. Place the muffin tins in oven.

Bake: Bake cupcakes until they spring back when lightly pressed with your finger and a toothpick inserted in the center comes out clean, about 20-25 minutes. Remove the muffin tins from oven and place on wire racks to cool for 5 minutes. Run a knife around the edges of the cupcake liners. Lift cupcakes up from the bottom of the tins using the end of the knife and carefully take them out of the cups with your fingertips. Place them on wire racks to cool for 15 minutes before frosting. Garnish with a peach slice.

Prep Frosting: Place margarine and 1 cup sugar in a large mixing bowl. Blend with mixer on low speed to incorporate, about 30 seconds. Add remaining sugar with 2 tablespoons soy milk and lemon juice. Blending with the mixer on low, stir in lemon zest. Add remaining tablespoon soy milk if frosting seems too stiff. Increase the mixer speed to medium and beat until light and fluffy, 1 more minute.

Frost Cakes: With a spatula, spread a heaping tablespoon of frosting on each cupcake until smooth. Top with a tablespoon of peach jam and garnish with fresh peaches.

prep time
15 minutes

cook time
45-50 minutes

serves
8-10

plan ahead
Cake may be
frozen up to
1 month.

fresh blueberry cake
with crumb topping

The quintessential coffee cake studded with fresh blueberries and a crumb topping…an irresistible treat for brunch or any time of the day!

- ⅓ cup (5½ tablespoons) butter or margarine, **softened**
- 1 cup sugar
- 2 cups flour
- 1 tablespoon baking powder
- 1 teaspoon salt
- 1 cup milk or soy milk
- 1 egg
- 1 pint blueberries, **rinsed, stems discarded**

crumb topping
- 1 cup flour
- ½ cup sugar
- 1 teaspoon cinnamon
- ¼ cup (½ stick) butter or margarine, **softened**

Prep: Preheat oven to 350°. Grease a tube pan or a 9x13-inch pan.

Mix: In the bowl of a standing electric mixer, cream butter or margarine and sugar together until well blended. Alternating between dry and wet ingredients, slowly add remaining ingredients (except for blueberries), beating until incorporated and mixture is smooth. Pour half of batter into the prepared pan. Sprinkle half of blueberries over batter. Repeat with remaining batter and blueberries.

Topping: In a small bowl, mix all topping ingredients together with your fingertips to form a coarse meal. Sprinkle evenly over cake.

Bake: If baking cake in a 9x13-inch pan, bake for 50 minutes, checking with a toothpick if done after 45 minutes. If baking in a tube pan, bake for 1 hour, checking with a toothpick after 50 minutes. If needed, bake 5 minutes more.

lemon-pomegranate ice cream bombes

Frozen desserts are a great do-ahead choice for entertaining and are an especially refreshing finish to a meal on a hot day. Be sure to start up to 2 days ahead.

prep time
40 minutes plus
freezing time
serves
6

- ½ cup sugar
- 1½ teaspoons packed finely grated lemon zest, plus more for garnish
- ¼ cup fresh lemon juice (from 2 large lemons)
- 2 large egg yolks
- ⅛ teaspoon salt
- ½ cup chilled whipping cream or frozen, non-dairy dessert whip topping, defrosted
- 1 quart vanilla ice cream, slightly softened
- ¾ cup pomegranate sorbet
- 2 cups fresh strawberries, chopped
- Pomegranate seeds

  garnish
- Mint sprigs

simplify

Substitute purchased lemon ice cream for vanilla ice cream and skip the step for lemon cream. Fill with pomegranate sorbet. This recipe also works well with strawberry or raspberry sorbet.

Lemon cream: Bring a pot of water to a boil over medium heat. Meanwhile, whisk sugar, zest, lemon juice, yolks and salt to blend in a medium bowl. Place the bowl over a pot of simmering water (do not allow the bottom of the bowl to touch water). Continue to whisk until mixture thickens, about 10 minutes. Refrigerate until cold, about 45 minutes. In a separate medium bowl, use electric beaters to beat cream until stiff peaks form. Gently fold whipped cream or topping into lemon mixture. Cover and refrigerate at least 6 hours and up to 1 day.

Layer: Line 6 (6-ounce) custard cups with foil, leaving a generous overhang. Place ½ cup plus 1 tablespoon ice cream in each custard cup. Using the back of a teaspoon, smooth an even layer of ice cream on bottom and up sides of cup, creating a hollow in center. Dip spoon in warm water as needed. Reserve unused ice cream for another use. Freeze ice cream cups for 1 hour. Spoon 2 tablespoons sorbet into the hollow in center of each cup and pack firmly. Return cups to freezer for 1 hour. Divide lemon cream among cups, smoothing tops. Freeze 3 hours. Slightly re-soften unused ice cream and spread 2 tablespoons ice cream over lemon cream in each cup, smoothing to cover completely. Fold foil overhang over bombes to cover; freeze at least 3 hours and up to 2 days.

Serve: Open foil on bombes; turn bombes upside down onto dishes. Peel off foil. Spoon fresh strawberries and pomegranate seeds alongside bombes. Garnish with mint sprigs and lemon zest.

Serving Option: This recipe can also be made layered as a terrine in a loaf pan.

prep time
30 minutes

cook time
2 hours

serves
8-10

plan ahead
Cheesecake can be made up to 1 week ahead and also freezes beautifully.

chocolate nut cheesecake with caramel sauce

A kid's dream come true, chocolate bars stud this cheesecake blanketed in sweet caramel… a treat for all ages!

cream cheese filling

- 4 (8-ounce) bars cream cheese, softened
- 3 tablespoons unsalted butter, softened
- 2¼ cups packed brown sugar
- 5 large eggs
- ¾ cup sour cream
- 3 candy bars (total 6.5 ounces) filled with nuts and caramel (e.g., Hershey's Nutrageous or Paskesz's Smirk), broken into pieces

graham cracker crust

- 2 cups graham cracker crumbs
- 3 tablespoons packed light brown sugar
- 6 tablespoons unsalted butter, melted

garnish

- Purchased caramel sauce
- 1 (3½-ounce) bittersweet chocolate bar, shaved into curls

Prep: Preheat oven to 300°. Grease a 10x3-inch springform pan. Using heavy duty foil, wrap the outside of the pan with foil.

Crust: In a medium bowl, stir together graham cracker crumbs, brown sugar and melted butter until well combined. Spread mixture evenly on the bottom of the prepared pan, pressing down firmly. Set aside.

Cream cheese filling: Using an electric mixer, beat cream cheese and butter at medium speed in a large bowl until creamy and well blended, about 1 minute. Add brown sugar and continue beating until combined. Reduce mixer to low speed, adding eggs one at a time, beating until incorporated. Add sour cream and blend. Add broken candy bars, beating for 15-20 seconds, until candy bars are broken up. Pour mixture into the prepared pan and place into a large roasting pan. Fill roasting pan with hot water until it comes halfway up the sides of the springform pan.

Bake: Bake for about 2 hours, until center has set completely and top is golden brown. Remove cake from the roasting pan and set on a wire rack until it comes to room temperature. Cover and refrigerate for a few hours or overnight. Prior to serving, carefully release and remove the sides of the springform pan.

Garnish: Warm caramel sauce slightly in the microwave. Pour over cooled cheesecake, covering top and letting it drip down sides. Decorate with shaved chocolate curls.

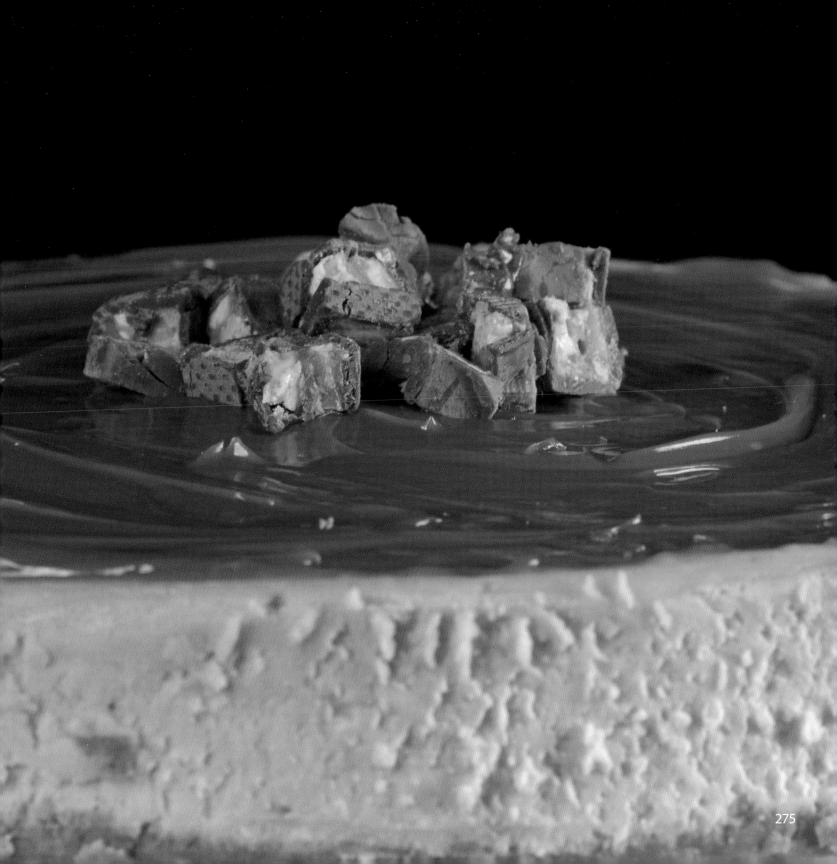

butterscotch ice cream
with nut-crunch topping

This smooth and creamy non-dairy ice cream has a rich buttery flavor, topped by an irresistible crunch.

prep time
15 minutes

cook time
5 minutes plus
20 minutes for
topping

serves
8

- 3 eggs
- ¼ teaspoon salt
- ⅔ cup dark brown sugar
- ¼ cup (½ stick) margarine
- 2 (8-ounce) containers frozen non-dairy dessert whip topping, defrosted
- 2 teaspoons vanilla sugar
- 1 cup toasted almonds, chopped (optional)
- Nut-crunch topping *(recipe below)*

plan ahead
Nut-crunch topping can be prepared 2 days ahead and stored in a tightly sealed container.

Ice cream: Place eggs and salt in a medium metal bowl; using an electric mixer, beat on high speed for 5-10 minutes until consistency is thick and custardy. Combine brown sugar and margarine in a small saucepan; place over medium heat until melted, mixing constantly. Remove from fire; set aside to cool slightly. Add whipped topping and vanilla sugar to eggs and beat for 2-3 minutes. Gently fold in the brown sugar mixture and toasted almonds.

Freeze: Transfer mixture to a large airtight container and freeze for at least 6 hours or overnight.

nut-crunch topping

- 1 cup flour
- ¼ cup dark brown sugar
- ½ cup nuts
- ½ cup (1 stick) margarine, melted

Preheat oven to 350°. In a medium bowl, combine all ingredients and mix well. Spread mixture evenly onto a greased cookie sheet and bake for 20 minutes. Break up into small pieces and sprinkle over ice cream.

prep time
40 minutes

cook time
45 minutes

serves
8-10

plan ahead

Finished dish can be made up to 2 days ahead. Cover and store in the refrigerator. Prior to serving, bring to room temperature and reheat.

melted chocolate bread pudding with spiced whipped cream

Hidden deep within is a decadent ripple of melted chocolate nestled between two layers of thick, rich chocolate bread pudding...the secret to this luscious dessert and the reason you'll be asking for seconds!

- 1 tablespoon butter or margarine, melted
- 2¼ cups milk or soy milk
- ⅓ cup brandy
- 3 cups (18 ounces) good quality chocolate chips, divided
- ½ cup packed dark brown sugar
- 1 teaspoon Chinese five-spice powder, divided
- 4 large eggs
- 1 teaspoon vanilla extract
- 8 slices of soft white bread, crust removed, cut into ½-inch cubes (about 6 cups)
- 2 cups whipping cream or frozen non-dairy dessert whip topping, defrosted
- 2 tablespoons sugar
- ½ teaspoon instant coffee

Prep: Grease a 9x13-inch oven-to-table baking dish with melted butter or margarine; set aside. Bring milk or soy milk and brandy to a simmer over medium-low heat in a heavy, large saucepan and cook for about 3 minutes. Remove from heat. Add 1 cup chocolate chips. Let stand for 1 minute and whisk until chocolate is melted and mixture is smooth. Whisk in brown sugar and ½ teaspoon five-spice powder. Let stand until cool, about 20 minutes. Add eggs, and then vanilla, and whisk to blend. Stir in bread. Let stand for 30 minutes.

Assemble: Spread half of bread mixture (about 2½ cups) into the prepared baking dish. Sprinkle remaining 2 cups chocolate chips evenly over mixture. Cover with remaining pudding mixture. At this point, dish can be made a day ahead; cover and store in the refrigerator.

Bake: Preheat oven to 350°. Bake pudding uncovered until puffed and firm in center, about 45 minutes. Check for doneness; remove from oven and cool for 10 minutes.

Whipped Cream: Using an electric mixer, beat whipping cream or whip topping, sugar, instant coffee and remaining five-spice powder in a medium bowl until peaks form.

Serve: Spoon pudding into bowls. Top with whipped cream.

mixed berry pavlovas

Named after the Russian ballerina Anna Pavlova, a Pavlova consists of a crisp meringue base topped with whipped cream and mixed fruit.

- 6 egg whites (from extra-large eggs)
- ¼ teaspoon cream of tartar
- Kosher salt
- 1½ cups sugar, divided
- ½ teaspoon vanilla extract
- 3 pints assorted berries (strawberries should be cut into small pieces)
- Fresh mint, chopped
- 1 tablespoon sugar
- 2 teaspoons fresh lemon juice
- 1 cup whipped cream

Prep: Preheat oven to 200°. Line 2 baking sheets with parchment paper. Using a small glass (approximately 3½ inches in diameter) and a pencil, trace 6 circles on each piece of parchment paper. Turn the parchment paper face down on the baking sheets.

Beat: In the bowl of a standing electric mixer fitted with the whisk attachment, beat egg whites, cream of tartar and large pinch of salt on medium speed until frothy. Add 1 cup sugar and raise the speed to high, beating until egg whites form very stiff peaks. Whisk in vanilla. Carefully whisk remaining sugar into meringue.

Shape: With a large star-shaped pastry tip, pipe a flat round of meringue inside each circle. Pipe a border of meringue around the edge to form sides of pavlovas shells.

Bake: Bake for 2 hours, or until pavlovas are dry and crisp but not browned. Turn off oven; leave meringues in oven for at least 4 hours or overnight.

Berry Sauce: Mix berries with chopped mint, sugar and lemon juice in a medium bowl. Let sit for 30 minutes.

Serve: Top each meringue with a dollop of whipped cream and a spoonful of berry topping.

prep time
40 minutes

cook time
2 hours plus
4 hours

yields
12 meringues

plan ahead

Berry sauce can be prepared a day ahead and stored in tightly covered container in the refrigerator.

cinnamon crumb cake

A good crumb cake with a fine moist crumb is hard to come by. The solution: a cinnamon-brown sugar ripple that runs through the coffee cake, providing a boost of sweet moistness.

- 1 cup oil
- 2 cups sugar
- 4 eggs
- 1 cup orange juice
- 1 teaspoon vanilla extract
- 3 cups flour
- 1 tablespoon baking powder
- 1¼ teaspoons cocoa
- ¾ teaspoon cinnamon
- ½ cup brown sugar

streusel topping
- ½ cup (1 stick) butter or margarine, cubed
- ½ cup flour
- ¼ cup sugar

Prep: Preheat oven to 375°. Grease a tube pan.

Mix: In the bowl of a standing electric mixer, cream oil and sugar. Add eggs, orange juice and vanilla, beating until well combined. Add flour and baking powder a little at a time, beating well in between additions. Scrape down the sides of the bowl. Beat for about 2 minutes; batter should be thick and smooth. Pour a third of batter into the prepared tube pan.

Fill: In a small bowl, combine cocoa, cinnamon and brown sugar; whisk to blend. Sprinkle half of mixture over batter in the tube pan. Layer another third of batter into the pan, then the remaining cinnamon mixture, topping with the remaining batter.

Topping: In a small bowl, combine topping ingredients. Blend with your fingertips to form a coarse meal. Set aside.

Bake: Place pan in oven and bake for 20 minutes. Remove from oven and evenly sprinkle streusel topping over batter. Bake for another 30 minutes, checking for doneness with a toothpick.

chocolate semifreddo
with candied orange sauce

Semifreddo literally means partially frozen, as is the chocolate mousse presented here. Dark, rich chocolate and sweet, tangy oranges are a classic dessert combination, but finishing the dish with candied oranges spikes the flavor to the next level!

prep time
40 minutes
cook time
10 minutes
serves
8

- 1¼ cups (2½ sticks) butter or margarine
- 10 ounces bittersweet chocolate, chopped
- 12 egg yolks
- 1 cup sugar
- 9 egg whites
- Candied Orange Sauce *(recipe below)*

Prep: Grease an 8½x5½x3-inch loaf pan with cooking spray, and line tightly with foil.

Semifreddo: Heat butter or margarine and chocolate in a medium saucepan over low heat. Stir until melted and mixture is uniform and smooth; remove from heat and set aside to cool. Meanwhile, combine egg yolks and sugar in the bowl of a standing electric mixer. Beat on high until sugar is dissolved and mixture is thick and pale yellow in color. Add chocolate mixture, mixing until combined. Set aside. In a separate large bowl, beat egg whites on high until stiff peaks form (avoid beating to dry point). Using a rubber spatula, gently fold egg whites into chocolate mixture (this can be done in batches) until combined. Pour into the prepared loaf pan and freeze, tightly covered.

Serve: Remove semifreddo from freezer and turn out onto plate; peel off foil. Cut into ¾-inch-thick slices and place on individual plates. Spoon warm orange sauce over slices and serve immediately.

plan ahead

Semifreddo can be prepared up to 2 weeks ahead and stored in the freezer. Candied orange sauce can be made up to 2 days ahead. Store in refrigerator, covered well. Rewarm before serving.

candied orange sauce

- 6 oranges, unpeeled, quartered and sliced into ¼-inch thick pieces
- ½ cup water
- ⅓ cup sugar
- 2 teaspoons orange liqueur
- 1 tablespoon fresh lemon juice
- 2½ teaspoons cornstarch
- ½ teaspoon grated orange peel

Combine all ingredients in a medium saucepan over medium heat. Cook, stirring often, until sauce begins to boil and thicken, about 5 minutes. Cool slightly.

chocolate tart with toasted hazelnuts

Simple to prepare and elegant to behold, this tart is also a delicious gluten-free option for dessert.

- 2¼ cups whole hazelnuts plus more for garnish
- ⅓ cup sugar
- ¼ cup (½ stick) butter or margarine, melted
- 1½ cups whipping cream or frozen
  non-dairy whip topping, defrosted
- 12 ounces semisweet chocolate, chopped

garnish
- 1 pint berries

Crust: Preheat oven to 350°. Place hazelnuts on a cookie sheet and toast for 5 minutes, shaking pan after 2 minutes. Remove from oven and let cool. Place hazelnuts and sugar in a food processor and chop until finely ground. Remove ½ cup nut mixture and set aside. Add butter to hazelnut mixture and mix until well combined. Press into sides and bottom of a large tart pan. Bake for 25 minutes.

Chocolate filling: Heat whipping cream in a small saucepan over medium heat until scalding (do not bring to a boil). Remove from heat and add chocolate; let sit for 2 minutes. Stir continuously until chocolate is completely melted and mixture is smooth. Let cool slightly; pour into hazelnut crust, spreading evenly. Arrange reserved hazelnut mixture in a large circle in center of tart. Place whole hazelnuts around border of tart. Finish with circle of berries inside hazelnut border.

peach strawberry mousse cake

Looking for your next summer centerpiece? Airy yet rich, luscious and ephemeral, this silky mousse cake is a perfect way to end a fine summer's meal.

p...
1 h...
chillin...
serves
12

mousse cake
- 1 (16-ounce) package vanilla sandwich cookies
- 1½ teaspoons grated lemon zest
- 1 tablespoon butter
- 1 (16-ounce) can peaches in light syrup, drained
- 3 (½-pint) containers fresh or frozen strawberries
- 2½ cups heavy whipping cream, divided
- 9 large egg yolks
- ¾ cup sugar

- ⅓ cup light corn syrup
- 2 tablespoons (¼ stick) unsalted butter, at room temperature
- 2 tablespoons peach schnapps

compote and topping
- 12 canned peach halves, thinly sliced
- ¼ cup sugar
- ⅓ cup peach schnapps
- 2 teaspoons fresh lemon juice
- 3 (½-pint) containers small strawberries

cook's note
Fresh peaches can be used for mousse cake. Use 3-4 large ripe peaches, peeled and cubed. Pureé the peaches, bring to a boil and cook uncovered for about 10 minutes over low flame until slightly reduced. Proceed with recipe.

Crust: Grease a 9-inch springform pan. Finely grind cookies, lemon zest and 1 tablespoon butter in a food processor fitted with the "S" blade. Press half of mixture over bottom of the prepared pan.

Purée: Purée peaches in a food processor until smooth; refrigerate. Purée strawberries in a food processor. Strain through a fine sieve set over a medium bowl, pressing to extract as much fruit as possible. Discard solids; refrigerate purée.

Mousse base: Combine ¼ cup cream, egg yolks, sugar, corn syrup and 2 tablespoons butter in a large metal bowl. Whisk to blend. Set bowl over a saucepan of simmering water over medium-low heat (do not allow the bottom of the bowl to touch water). Whisk constantly until mousse base thickens and thermometer inserted into base registers 160°F, about 10 minutes. Remove the bowl from the saucepan. Using an electric mixer, beat mousse base until thickened and billowy, about 8 minutes. Divide mixture between 2 medium bowls (about 1 cup mousse base in each bowl). Beat remaining 2¼ cups cream in a separate large bowl until medium peaks form. Set aside.

Peach mousse: Fold 1 cup chilled peach purée and schnapps into 1 mousse base, and then fold in half of whipped cream. Spread peach mousse in the prepared pan. Sprinkle remaining cookie mixture over mousse and freeze.

Strawberry mousse: Fold 1 cup strawberry purée (reserve remaining purée for another use) into mousse base in the second bowl. Fold in remaining whipped cream. Spread strawberry mousse over cookie mixture in pan. Cover; freeze at least 8 hours and up to 2 days.

Compote and topping: Combine all ingredients except strawberries in a large bowl; let compote stand at room temperature at least 15 minutes and up to 1 hour, stirring occasionally. Arrange strawberries on top of cake.

Serve: Cut cake into wedges. Spoon compote over strawberries.

biscotti
with chocolate and pistachios

...otti is the perfect "dunker"—crisp and firm enough to hold up when dipped into a tea or dessert.
...ar to Jewish Mandlebrodt, this twice-baked Italian cookie has a great shelf life.

rep time
our plus
g time

...container,
biscotti can be
made up to a week
ahead.

- ...up sugar
- 1 cup canola oil
- 2 teaspoons baking powder
- 1 tablespoon vanilla sugar
- 4 cups flour
- 1 (12-ounce) bag mini chocolate chips
- ¼ cup shelled pistachios, chopped
- 1 (3½-ounce) white chocolate bar, roughly chopped
- Cinnamon and sugar, for dusting

Prep: Preheat oven to 350°. Line 2 cookie sheets with parchment paper; set aside.

Beat: Using an electric mixer, beat eggs and sugar together in a large bowl for 3-4 minutes. Add oil, baking powder and vanilla sugar and beat 2-3 minutes. Add flour, mixing slowly to incorporate. Mix in chocolate chips, pistachios and white chocolate chunks.

Shape: Divide mixture into 2 portions and place each onto the prepared cookie sheets. Using your hands, shape into 2 long, flat logs. Sprinkle each with cinnamon and sugar and bake for 30 minutes. Remove from oven and let cool for 10-15 minutes. When cool enough to touch, use a sharp knife to slice crosswise into long, thin strips, about ¼-inch thick. Lay each slice flat on the cookie sheets in an even layer. Return to oven to bake for 10 minutes more on each side until lightly browned and firm.

skillet blueberry bake

This dessert is perfect in any season. Summer fresh blueberries could not taste any better, but even with frozen blueberries on a cold winter's night, the spiced blueberries will warm your meal right up.

prep time
10 minutes
cook time
40 minutes
serves
6-8

filling
- 4 cups fresh blueberries (from 2 pints), **picked over**
- ½ cup packed light brown sugar
- ¼ cup mild-flavored (light) molasses or corn syrup
- ¼ cup water
- 2 teaspoons finely grated lemon zest
- 3 tablespoons fresh lemon juice (from about 2 lemons)
- ¼ teaspoon ground nutmeg
- ¼ teaspoon ground cloves

topping
- 3 cups flour
- ¼ cup sugar
- 4 teaspoons baking powder
- 1 teaspoon salt
- 6 tablespoons chilled unsalted butter or margarine, **cut into ¼-inch cubes**
- 1½ cups milk or soy milk

cook's note

This dish looks very rustic and homey. Table-side serving is recommended as this dish cannot be removed from the pan and transferred whole for serving.

Frozen blueberries may be used. Defrost and proceed with directions.

Filling: Mix all ingredients in a 12-inch skillet. Bring to a boil over medium-high heat, stirring until sugar dissolves. Reduce heat to medium; simmer until berries soften and mixture thickens slightly, about 10 minutes. Meanwhile, prepare topping.

Topping: Whisk flour, sugar, baking powder and salt in a medium bowl to blend. Add butter or margarine and rub with fingertips until mixture resembles fine meal. Add milk or soy milk; stir just until blended and sticky dough forms. Drop batter by tablespoonfuls onto the simmering berry mixture, placing dough close together (you may have leftover topping). Reduce heat to medium-low; cover skillet and simmer until topping is firm and toothpick inserted comes out clean, about 25 minutes.

Serving Option: For a prettier presentation, place all filling ingredients in a decorative oven-to-table baking dish and bake at 350° for about 20 minutes, covered, stirring halfway through. Place topping over blueberries and bake for 40 more minutes.

prep time
15 minutes

cook time
15-20 minutes

yields
24 cupcakes

mexican chocolate cupcakes with cinnamon coffee frosting

These are not ordinary chocolate cupcakes. A hint of fire and spice is in each bite… Buyer-beware!

- 2 cups all-purpose flour
- ¾ cup unsweetened cocoa powder
- 1 cup sugar
- 1 teaspoon baking soda
- 2 teaspoons ground cinnamon
- ½ teaspoon cayenne pepper
- Pinch of salt
- ¾ cup vegetable oil
- 1 cup water
- 2 eggs
- ½ cup buttermilk
- Cinnamon Coffee Frosting *(recipe below)*

Prepare: Preheat oven to 350°. Grease cupcake tins with cooking spray.

Mix: Combine flour, cocoa, sugar, baking soda, cinnamon, cayenne pepper and salt in a large bowl. Whisk to blend. Add oil, water, eggs and buttermilk. Mix until smooth. Pour into prepared cupcake tins, filling each halfway.

Bake: Bake for 15-20 minutes until toothpick inserted comes out clean. Remove from oven and transfer cupcake tins to cooling racks.

Frost: When cool, carefully remove each cupcake from tin. Frost with Cinnamon Coffee Frosting *(recipe below)*.

Serving Option: Recipe can also be made as one large cake; increase baking time to 30 minutes.

simplify

Cake: *No time to bake from scratch? Combine devil's food cake mix with 2 teaspoons cinnamon, ¼ teaspoon cayenne powder and 1 tablespoon balsamic vinegar. Continue according to package directions.*

Frosting: *Use purchased vanilla frosting mixed with 1 teaspoon espresso powder and ½ teaspoon cinnamon.*

cook's note

For non-dairy buttermilk, mix ½ cup vanilla soy milk and 1 tablespoon balsamic vinegar. Let sit for 2-3 minutes; mixture will curdle.

cinnamon coffee frosting

- ½ cup (1 stick) butter or margarine, softened
- 1 teaspoon instant espresso powder
- ½ teaspoon ground cinnamon
- Pinch of salt
- 1 teaspoon vanilla extract
- 3 cups confectioner's sugar
- 2-3 tablespoons milk

Using an electric mixer, beat butter or margarine in a medium bowl until smooth. Add espresso powder, cinnamon, salt and vanilla, beating until incorporated. Alternately beat in confectioner's sugar and milk until desired consistency is achieved.

mini apple tarts tatin

Imagine an upside-down caramelized apple pie with a crisp crust on the bottom. Then you can understand the beauty of the French tart tatin. This version uses a muffin pan for perfect individual servings.

prep time
30 minutes

cook time
40 minutes

serves
12

- 8 ounces frozen puff pastry dough, thawed
- ½ cup water
- 1½ cups sugar
- 1½ teaspoons honey
- 6 tablespoons butter or margarine, cut into ½-inch pieces
- 2 pounds apples (4-5 apples), peeled, cored and thinly sliced
- Whipped cream (optional)

Prep: Preheat oven to 400°. Lightly grease the inside of a 12-cup muffin tin set on a rimmed baking sheet.

Dough: Place puff pastry dough on a lightly floured surface and use a 3-inch round cookie cutter to cut out 12 circles. Place circles on a tray and prick with a fork. Chill for 10 minutes in the refrigerator.

Sauce: Pour water into a medium saucepan and place over medium heat. Add sugar and honey, and increase to high heat. Swirling the pan occasionally, boil until sugar turns a dark amber color, about 10-12 minutes. Remove the pan from heat and whisk in butter or margarine, 1 piece at a time, until completely melted and emulsified. Divide sauce among the muffin cups.

Bake: Divide apple slices among the muffin cups, breaking them in half when necessary to pack in all the slices. Top each muffin cup with a circle of puff pastry dough. Bake for 20 minutes, and then reduce temperature to 350° and continue baking until pastry is golden brown and apples are tender when pricked with a fork, another 20-25 minutes.

Serve: Transfer the muffin tin to a wire rack to cool for 20-30 minutes. Use a spoon to help lift out tarts, inverting (apple side up) and transferring to a platter. Alternatively, let tarts cool and reheat in a 350° oven for 5-10 minutes before inverting onto a serving platter. Serve with whipped cream, if desired.

Serving Option: Recipe can be made as a large 9-inch-round tart.

prep time
5 minutes plus chilling time

cook time
5 minutes

serves
4-6

cook's note
While the liqueur can be omitted, it adds to the rich flavor of the sorbets.

pina colada sorbet

- 1 cup superfine sugar
- 1 cup water
- 1 (20-ounce) can crushed pineapple, drained
- 1 (14-ounce) can coconut milk
- ¼ cup lime juice
- 3 tablespoons vodka
- ⅛ cup shredded unsweetened coconut (optional)

Simple syrup: Combine sugar and water in a small saucepan and bring to a boil over high heat for 1 minute or until sugar is dissolved (liquid will become clear). Set aside to cool.

Purée: Blend pineapple in a blender until very smooth and frothy. Combine pineapple purée, cooled syrup, coconut milk, lime juice and vodka in a large bowl. Whisk to blend. Refrigerate until chilled, about 1-2 hours. Pour into an ice cream maker and follow manufacturer's directions.

Freeze: Transfer to an airtight container and freeze overnight.

Mango

Pina Colada

kiwi sorbet

prep time
10 minutes plus chilling time

serves
4

- 12 very ripe kiwis, **peeled**
- 1 cup superfine sugar
- Zest of ¼ lime (½ teaspoon)
- Juice of one lime
- ⅓ cup white wine

cook's note

To ripen kiwis, place in a brown bag with a banana for a day.

Blend: Blend all ingredients in a blender until smooth. Strain half of pureé through a fine mesh sieve to remove seeds, use a rubber spatula or wooden spoon to press solids and extract as much liquid as possible. Discard seeds. Add strained kiwi back into remaining pureé. Pour into an ice cream maker and follow manufacturer's directions.

Freeze: Transfer to an airtight container and freeze overnight.

Non-Alcoholic Option: For a child-friendly version, omit wine and replace with ginger ale.

mango tango sorbet

prep time
15 minutes plus chilling time

serves
4

- 3 large mangoes, cubed (4 cups)
- ½ cup mango nectar
- 1 tablespoon orange liqueur (like Triple Sec)
- 1½ teaspoons fresh grated ginger or 1 frozen ginger cube (optional)
- ½ cup sugar

Blend: Blend mango, nectar, liqueur and ginger in a blender on medium speed until smooth. Add sugar and blend until sugar is dissolved. Pour into an ice cream maker and follow manufacturer's directions.

Freeze: Transfer to an airtight container and freeze overnight.

Kiwi

prep time
20 minutes

cook time
1 hour

serves
16

plan ahead

*Cake freezes
beautifully and will
also stay fresh if
stored covered, at
room temperature,
for up to 5 days.*

chocolate kahlua cake

EXCERPTED FROM *CHOCOLATE BY THE CAKE MIX DOCTOR*, COPYRIGHT 2001 BY ANNE BYRN.
USED BY PERMISSION OF WORKMAN PUBLISHING CO., INC. NEW YORK. ALL RIGHTS RESERVED.

*Using a cake mix makes this recipe a snap to prepare. The end result is a cake so perfect in flavor
and texture that you will make this every week!*

- 1 (18.25-ounce) package golden butter-recipe cake mix
- 1 (3.9-ounce) package chocolate instant pudding mix
- 1 cup sour cream or non-dairy sour cream
- ½ cup (1 stick) butter or margarine, melted
- ½ cup vegetable oil
- 4 large eggs
- 7 tablespoons coffee liqueur, divided
- 1 teaspoon pure vanilla extract
- 1 cup semisweet chocolate chips

  garnish
- 1 tablespoon confectioner's sugar, sifted

Prep: Place oven rack in center of oven and preheat to 350°. Lightly mist a 12-cup bundt
pan with cooking oil spray, and then dust with flour. Shake out excess flour. Set aside.

Mix: Place cake mix, pudding mix, sour cream, melted butter or margarine, oil, eggs,
4 tablespoons of liqueur and vanilla in a large bowl. Blend with an electric mixer on low
speed for 1 minute. Stop the mixer and scrape down the sides with a spatula. Increase the
speed to medium and beat for 2 more minutes, scraping down the sides again if needed.
Batter should look thick and well combined. Fold in chocolate chips, making sure they are
well distributed throughout batter. Pour batter into the prepared pan, smoothing it out with
a spatula.

Bake: Bake until cake springs back when lightly pressed with your finger and is just starting to
pull away from the sides of the pan, 55-60 minutes. Insert a toothpick into cake's center and
make sure it comes out clean before removing cake from oven. Place cake on a wire rack to cool
for 20 minutes. Run a long, sharp knife around the edge of the cake and invert it onto a rack.

With a wooden skewer, poke holes in top of cake. Spoon remaining 3 tablespoons liqueur over
cake, letting it seep down into the holes. Let cake cool completely for 20 more minutes.

Place cake on a serving platter; dust with confectioner's sugar. Slice and serve.

raspberry swirl brownies

Take your brownies to the next level with this Cake Mix Doctor recipe – quick and easy, it's a great go-to dessert when short on time.

prep time
10 minutes

cook time
25 minutes

yields
24 squares

- 1 (19.8-ounce) package brownie mix
- ½ cup (1 stick) unsalted butter, melted
- ⅓ cup water
- 2 large eggs
- 1 teaspoon vanilla extract
- ½ cup seedless raspberry jam
- ¼ cup semisweet chocolate chips
- ½ cup pecans, finely chopped (optional)

Prepare: Place a rack in the center of oven and preheat to 350°. Lightly grease the bottom of a 9x13-inch pan with cooking spray. Set the pan aside.

Mix: Place brownie mix, melted butter, water, eggs and vanilla in a large mixing bowl. Mix until all ingredients are incorporated and batter lightens in texture, about 1-2 minutes. Pour batter into the prepared pan, smoothing it out with a rubber spatula. Drop raspberry jam by teaspoonfuls onto batter, and with a knife, swirl jam into batter. Scatter chocolate chips and pecans evenly over top. Place the pan in oven.

Bake: Bake brownies until outer 2 inches form a crust and feel firm, about 23-27 minutes. Remove the pan from oven and transfer to a cooling rack. Cool completely, about 30 minutes. Slice and serve brownies.

Serving Option: Serve with raspberry-mocha coffee for a truly delectable finish to any meal. Add 1 tablespoon raspberry syrup and 1½ tablespoons chocolate syrup to hot coffee with milk and top with whipped cream and a brownie chunk.

prep time
30 minutes

cook time
15 minutes

yields
3 dozen
cookies

plan ahead

*Fillings may be
made 1 week
ahead and stored
in an airtight
container in
the refrigerator.
Bring filling to
room temperature
before use.*

french macaroons with three fillings

*Stylish and pretty, these one-bite wonders have taken the dessert world by storm.
Mix and match your favorites!*

- 2 cups confectioner's sugar
- 1 cup (lightly packed) almond flour*
- ½ cup egg whites (from about 3 large eggs)
- 2 tablespoons plus ½ teaspoon sugar
- Your choice of fillings *(see page 306)*
  chocolate cinnamon ganache, banana crème and strawberry crème

Prep: Line 2 large baking sheets with parchment paper. Position oven racks on top and bottom shelves of the oven; preheat to 375°.

Beat: Sift confectioner's sugar and almond flour into a large bowl. Place egg whites, sugar and pinch of salt into another large bowl. Using an electric mixer, beat on high speed until stiff peaks form. Gently fold egg white mixture into almond mixture until incorporated. Spoon mixture into a pastry bag and pipe 1¼-inch rounds onto the prepared baking sheets, spacing 1 inch apart (this can also be done with a teaspoon). Let rest on sheets at room temperature for 20 minutes.

Bake: Bake cookies for 5 minutes. Reduce oven temperature to 325°. Continue to bake cookies until puffed and golden on top, about 10 minutes, rotating sheets in oven after 5 minutes. Transfer to cooling racks. Carefully peel cookies from parchment paper when cool.

Fill: Line a rimmed baking sheet with parchment paper. Spoon 1 scant teaspoon of filling onto the flat side of macaroon. Top with second macaroon, flat side down, pressing slightly to adhere and to gently press filling almost to edge of macaroon. Place on the prepared sheet. Repeat with remaining filling and macaroons. Cover and refrigerate overnight.

*Almond flour may also be called "almond meal" or "ground almonds" and can be found at specialty foods stores and natural foods stores. Look for blanched almond flour if available – it will yield a very fine texture. Almond flour can also be made at home by grinding whole almonds in a food processor until very fine.

plan ahead

*Fillings may be
made 1 week
ahead and stored
in an airtight
container in
the refrigerator.
Rewarm the
filling over very
low heat, stirring
occasionally.*

simplify

*For a simple
chocolate
ganache filling,
use a purchased
chocolate
hazelnut spread.*

chocolate cinnamon ganache filling

- ¾ cup heavy whipping cream or frozen, non-dairy dessert whip topping, **defrosted**
- ⅓ cup light brown sugar
- 6 ounces bittersweet chocolate, **chopped**
- ¼ cup (½ stick) unsalted butter or margarine, **softened**
- ½ teaspoon cinnamon

Combine whipping cream or whip topping and brown sugar in a small heavy saucepan. Bring mixture to a boil over medium-high heat, whisking occasionally, until brown sugar is dissolved. Remove the pan from the heat, add chocolate and whisk until mixture is melted and smooth. Add butter or margarine and cinnamon, whisking until filling is well blended; cool slightly.

banana crème filling

- ¾ cup heavy whipping cream or frozen, non-dairy dessert whip topping, **defrosted**
- 1 package vanilla pudding mix
- ¼ cup water
- 1 (4-ounce) jar banana baby food

Combine whipping cream or whip topping, pudding mix and water in a large bowl. Using an electric mixer, beat on medium speed until soft peaks form. Slowly add baby food, beating until well combined.

strawberry crème filling

- ⅓ cup seedless strawberry jelly
- ¾ cup heavy whipping cream or frozen, non-dairy dessert whip topping, **defrosted**
- 1 package vanilla pudding mix
- ¼ cup water

In a small saucepan, melt jelly over low heat until jelly liquifies. Let cool slightly. Combine whipping cream or whip topping, pudding mix and water in a large bowl. Using an electric mixer, beat on medium speed until soft peaks form. Slowly add melted jelly; gently mix to combine.

whole wheat oatmeal cookies with chocolate drizzle glaze

Finally, a healthy cookie you can feel good about serving (and eating!). Whole grains and oats yield a deliciously hearty cookie with a velvety chocolate glaze.

prep time
15 minutes
cook time
10-12 minutes
yields
30 cookies

- 1 egg
- 1 egg white
- ½ cup canola oil
- 1 cup sugar
- ½ cup brown sugar
- 1 teaspoon pure vanilla extract
- Pinch of salt

- 1 teaspoon baking soda
- 1½ cups whole wheat flour
- 1 (10-ounce) bag chocolate chips
- 1½ cups oats
- Chocolate drizzle

chocolate drizzle

- ½ cup cocoa
- ½ cup water
- 1 box confectioner's sugar

In a medium bowl, mix all ingredients to form a smooth, thick glaze.

Prep: Preheat oven to 350°. Line 2 cookie sheets with parchment paper; set aside.

Mix: Using an electric mixer, blend egg, egg white and oil together in a large mixing bowl until well combined. Add remaining ingredients and mix well. Place tablespoon-size mounds of cookie dough onto the prepared sheets, approximately 2 inches apart.

Bake: Bake cookies for about 11 minutes; do not overbake. Remove from oven and transfer to cooling racks.

Glaze: Pour thin amount of Chocolate Drizzle decoratively over top of cooled cookies.

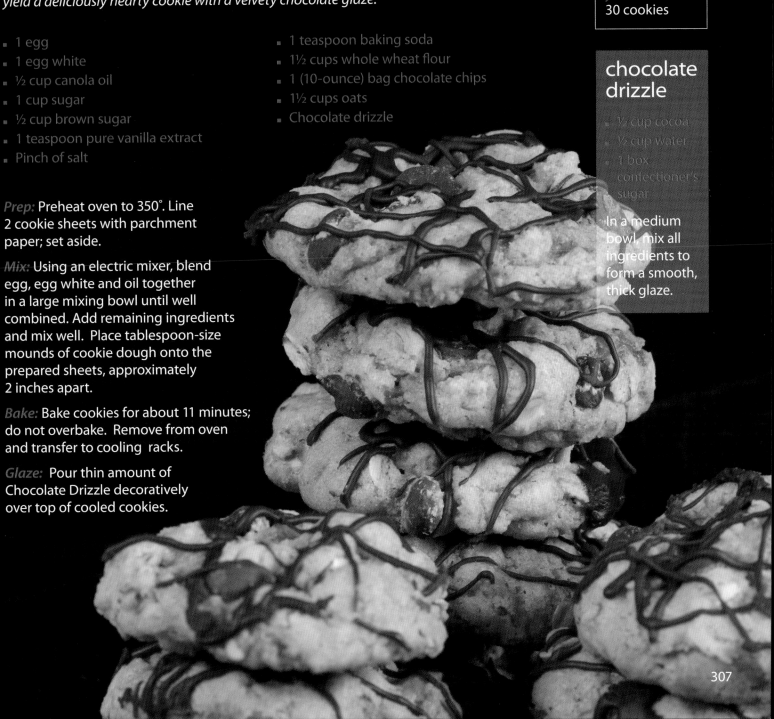

TORAH
ACADEMY
FOR GIRLS

Index